Endorsements

"When I need to look lean, I put great emphasis on eating healthy. The recipes and ab workouts in *The Everything® Flat Belly Cookbook* are exactly what I'd use to cut fat and define my abs."

—Cameron Mathison, Actor
All My Children, Dancing with the Stars

"Thank you Fitz for this amazing all-in-one book on how to combine a healthy lifestyle and workout routine with food that actually tastes great!! You've finally given pancakes, burgers, and barbecue ranch dressing a good reputation. Your versions of some very unhealthy foods are convenient, nutritious, and downright lip-smacking tasty! I will never eat the same again. You rock Fitz!"

—Colin Egglesfield, Actor
All My Children; Calvin Klein Model

"This is not just another diet book, but rather a detailed description to living the healthy lifestyle that will help you transform, achieve, and maintain the 'flat'tering figure you desire."

—Brandon Russell
Carpenter Host, *Trading Spaces*

"In *The Everything® Flat Belly Cookbook*, Fitz transfers her passion for fitness to readers with a full arsenal of recipes and workouts perfect for losing—and keeping off—unwanted pounds."

—Joe Cirulli, Past *IHRSA* President and Owner
of the *Gainesville Health & Fitness Centers*

"The recipes in *The Everything® Flat Belly Cookbook* are not only delicious, they're also easy to prepare—and good for you, too! The perfect book for anyone looking to drop some weight and tone their abs."

—Jeremy Foley
University of Florida Athletic Director

"Fitz will not only knock your socks off, but some body fat as well! Follow the advice of a true expert who practices what she preaches and will help you attain the fit and healthy body you've always wanted."

—Jose Antonio, PhD
CEO of the International Society of Sports Nutrition

"In 1998 the Florida Gator women's tennis team that I coached won the third national team title of that decade and Fitz was a big part of our success. Her work with the girls made them stronger both physically and mentally. *The Everything® Flat Belly Cookbook* will give you VIP access to an amazing trainer who will hold your hand on your path to better living."

—Andy Brandi, Professional Tennis Coach at The Solomon Institute
and Former University of Florida Women's Tennis Coach

"The combination of Fitz's fitness tips and healthy recipes in *The Everything® Flat Belly Cookbook* is guaranteed to get you in the best shape of your life!"

—Buddy Lee
U.S. Olympic Wrestler

"Fitz is the master of abdominal training. Live off the recipes in *The Everything® Flat Belly Cookbook*, do the ab exercises she prescribes, and dust off your skimpiest swimsuit and board shorts. You're going to want to live in them!"

—Tracy Benham, MS Exercise and Sport Physiologist;
Executive Producer, The Active Health Network
Director, Sports Health Exercise LLC

"*The Everything® Flat Belly Cookbook* is more than a simple collection of recipes . . . Fitz has created a down-to-earth guideline for living a healthier life."

—Marci Slayton, MD

THE
EVERYTHING®
FLAT BELLY COOKBOOK

Dear Reader,

I'm thrilled you've decided to allow me to help you earn a flat belly, and I'm eager to get started. I've been where you are, and it's no fun to feel less than fantastic about your body. Through my education and decades of experience I've figured things out and am finally elated with my abs. More importantly, I'm comfortable in my skin. Hooray!

I've trained millions of people over the past two decades and feel honored to have made a difference in their lives. Now it's time to affect yours. I need you to commit to fitness, because you will only reach your ambitious goals with discipline and continuous effort. This doesn't mean you have to train for a marathon, but you do have to be dedicated to making great choices.

I'm going to give you the exact formula for losing weight. This is not a diet! I'm just making you smarter, providing you with the tools (recipes) to make great choices, and then giving you a ton of little kicks in the tush to keep you going.

I'm not only an educator, I'm a cheerleader too. Send all of your success stories to me at Fitzness.com (*www.fitzness.com*) so I can congratulate you when you reach your goals. I am rooting for you. Now get to work!

Punches and kicks,

Welcome to the EVERYTHING® Series!

These handy, accessible books give you all you need to tackle a difficult project, gain a new hobby, comprehend a fascinating topic, prepare for an exam, or even brush up on something you learned back in school but have since forgotten.

You can choose to read an *Everything*® book from cover to cover or just pick out the information you want from our two useful boxes: e-facts and e-ssentials. We give you everything you need to know on the subject, but throw in a lot of fun stuff along the way, too.

We now have more than 400 *Everything*® books in print, spanning such wide-ranging categories as weddings, pregnancy, cooking, music instruction, foreign language, crafts, pets, New Age, and so much more. When you're done reading them all, you can finally say you know *Everything*®!

FACTS
Important snippets
of information

Quick
handy tips

PUBLISHER Karen Cooper

DIRECTOR OF ACQUISITIONS AND INNOVATION Paula Munier

MANAGING EDITOR, EVERYTHING SERIES Lisa Laing

COPY CHIEF Casey Ebert

ACQUISITIONS EDITOR Katrina Schroeder

ASSOCIATE DEVELOPMENT EDITOR Elizabeth Kassab

SENIOR DEVELOPMENT EDITOR Brett Palana-Shanahan

EDITORIAL ASSISTANT Hillary Thompson

Visit the entire Everything® series at *www.everything.com*

THE
EVERYTHING®
FLAT BELLY
COOKBOOK

300 quick and easy recipes
to help drop the belly fat
and tone your abs

Fitz Koehler, MSESS
with Mabelissa Acevedo, LDN

Aadamsmedia

Avon, Massachusetts

I dedicate this book to my gorgeous husband Rob and our beautiful little beans, Ginger and Parker. Mom, I'm extremely grateful for all of your help too!

———————

An *Everything® Series* Book.
Everything® and *everything.com®* are registered trademarks of F+W Media, Inc.

Published by Adams Media, a division of F+W Media, Inc.
57 Littlefield Street, Avon, MA 02322. U.S.A.
www.adamsmedia.com

ISBN 10: 1-60550-676-1
ISBN 13: 978-1-60550-676-0

Printed in the United States of America.

J I H G F E D C B A

Library of Congress Cataloging-in-Publication Data
is available from the publisher.

This publication is designed to provide accurate and authoritative information with regard to the subject matter covered. It is sold with the understanding that the publisher is not engaged in rendering legal, accounting, or other professional advice. If legal advice or other expert assistance is required, the services of a competent professional person should be sought.

—From a *Declaration of Principles* jointly adopted by a Committee of the American Bar Association and a Committee of Publishers and Associations

Many of the designations used by manufacturers and sellers to distinguish their products are claimed as trademarks. Where those designations appear in this book and Adams Media was aware of a trademark claim, the designations have been printed with initial capital letters.

Exercise photos in Chapter 1 courtesy of Matt Marriott.

This book is available at quantity discounts for bulk purchases.
For information, please call 1-800-289-0963.

Contents

Acknowledgments

This book was on my list of things to conquer, and I couldn't have done it without the support of my family and friends. To my husband Rob, thanks for allowing me the time I needed to make this happen. You are far better than I deserve. My little beans, Ginger and Parker: your perfect little hugs, kisses, and giggles elate me and remind me what I'm working for. Mom, your contributions and thoughtfulness have been really sweet. The word "grateful" just doesn't cut it for this situation.

To my literary agent, Grace Freedson, thanks for getting me this book deal. Now I want nine more. (My list of things to conquer is long!) Thanks to Mabelissa Acevedo. I adore, admire, and appreciate you more than you'll ever know. I love my friend and photographer, Matt Marriott of MattMarriott.org. Matt, you are deserving of complete loyalty. Thanks to Kristi, Tracy, Robin, Darcy, Leah, Jen, Wendy, Anita, Matt, Cindy, Jody, Suelen, Amy, Barry, Dawn, Susan, Jacki, Kristen, Jim, and all of the others who shared their favorite recipes with me. I am the luckiest girl in the world to have friends and family members like you.

Top Ten Things People with Flat Bellies Do

1. Count their calories.

2. Do challenging cardiovascular, strength, balance training, and flexibility exercises on a regular basis.

3. Spend some time every other day doing abdominal exercises.

4. Get most of their calories from produce and lean-protein sources.

5. Save desserts (even low-fat ones) for truly rare occasions.

6. Drink alcohol only a few times each year.

7. Avoid drinking almost any calories at all.

8. Reject excuses and commit to fitness.

9. Force healthy food and exercise into their lives while traveling.

10. Live a longer, more vibrant life!

Introduction

A flat, firm belly and strong abs are the status symbol of the day. It is the ultimate sign of overall fitness, and it tells others that you exercise, eat right, and take darn good care of yourself! Besides being attractive, the owners of flat bellies are far less likely to deal with a slew of unsavory health issues like type 2 diabetes, cancer, and heart disease. The great news is that earning a chiseled middle is not a very complicated task. You heard right! With a simple yet strategic plan for eating and a variety of well-rounded abdominal exercises, you too can whittle your middle and toss that girdle in the garbage.

The following is the formula for a flat belly: *Create a strong core (abdominal and back muscles) while losing any excess body fat you may have.* Tons of people have very strong abdominal muscles, yet they still boast bulging midsections. It doesn't matter how strong your abs are; if you are overweight your belly will not be flat. Once you change your eating habits with recipes like the ones included in this book, you'll be amazed at how quickly your waist will shrink and your abdominals will shine!

Eighty percent of weight loss comes as a result of wise food choices. That's why *The Everything® Flat Belly Cookbook* will prove to be such a valuable tool for you. The recipes included in it are low in fat and calories, high in fiber, and often packed with protein. This is a surefire formula to streamline your efforts in the kitchen. Many of the recipes are quick and easy to make, which is important in getting you to make them. Some of them are fancy and complicated, just so you can feel super savvy while hosting dinner parties.

Live off the recipes in this book for at least a few months, and choose restaurant meals that are similar to the recipes you find here. Eventually, eating for a flatter belly will come naturally to you. This is not a diet. These recipes are designed to provide you a variety of healthy choices to make a new lifestyle. Once you lose your extra body weight and your belly looks like that of a movie star, don't even consider going back to your old eating habits. They are gone forever. Adios, big-belly food!

On top of 300 recipes, you'll find photos and descriptions of some fabulous abdominal exercises. Your mission is to spend between five and fifteen minutes a day three times a week training your abdominal muscles from here on out. Achieving and maintaining a sturdy core will provide the perfect structure for a flat and toned waistline. You can also help the process along by aggressively pursuing a variety of challenging cardiovascular and strength-building exercises. Balance work and flexibility training are important as well.

A flat belly is the result of a big-picture attitude about health and fitness. If you truly want to earn and keep a flat belly, you're going to have to up the ante in all areas of your life. Eat better and sleep better. Elevate the difficulty and frequency of your workouts. Do this and the flat belly you earn will stick with you for a lifetime and make your life great!

Chapter 1
Flat Belly Philosophy

No matter how far from flat your belly may be, this book is your ticket to amazing abdominals. If you're looking for the secret to fighting fat and slimming your sides, you're about to hear it. Strangely enough, this "secret" is not so much a secret as it is a standard formula that's been wildly misconstrued and butchered. What the makers of abdominal training equipment don't want you to know is that crunches are not the most important factor affecting your waistline.

You Are What You Eat

Your eating habits are about 80 percent responsible for your weight. Period. Imagine how much weight you would lose if you were stranded on an island with no food for four days. Even without exercising, you'd probably lose at least 10 pounds. Now imagine how much exercise you would have to do in your regular life to lose 10 pounds. Losing 10 pounds without changing your eating habits would require you to burn 36,000 more calories than you consume. Eating normally, a 150-pound person would have to run about 360 miles to run off 10 pounds. So which seems more difficult to you—eating a bit less each day or running off tons of extra calories? Carefully selecting what you put in your mouth simply requires less effort than exercise.

Exercise is vital for true fitness. It shapes your body and builds strength, flexibility, stamina, and balance. Exercise is a crucial component of your health that should never be ignored, but changing your eating habits is an easier way to lose and manage your weight.

Blasting Belly Fat

The reason you're hearing about weight loss instead of abdominal exercise is because if your belly is not flat, it's covered with a layer of fat. Whether your layer is large or small, the formula for getting rid of it is still the same. Getting rid of a larger layer just takes longer. Burn more calories than you consume and eventually your body will become lean and free of excessive body fat. This formula will also cause your hips, thighs, chest, arms, and neck to become leaner as well. The title of the book doesn't brag about this fact, but if you adhere to the recipes and advice included, your entire body will become leaner.

This Is Not a Diet

That's where these recipes come in. This book does not condone dieting. No way; no how. Diets are temporary measures that usually lead to temporary results. This book provides you with a well-rounded, nutritious variety of low-calorie, low-fat, and high-fiber recipes to turn to throughout each day. Choosing these recipes will ensure that you not only eat healthfully but that you are physically satisfied by a smaller amount of calories.

Budgeting Calories

This book focuses on foods that offer a lot of bang for your caloric buck. For example, broccoli is full of fiber, very filling, and extremely low in calories. You could eat more than 3 cups of broccoli for less than 100 calories. Once you did this, your stomach would feel like it was going to burst and you wouldn't want another bite of food for a few hours. Isn't it great that you can truly fill your tummy for less than 100 calories? Lean meat is very similar. An entire cup of chopped, skinless, grilled chicken breast would only cost you about 230 calories, so it is also a very nutritious and low-calorie way to fill up!

On the flip side, one bagel could cost you as much as 400 calories while providing very little nutritional value. Not only that, but most folks are accustomed to topping their bagels with extra fat and calories, which would put them even further in the caloric hole.

FACT

Does all of this math sound familiar? It might if you are savvy with your finances. Choosing low-calorie food is very similar to shopping for good sales. Getting an entire meal for less than 400 calories is the equivalent of getting a great flat-screen TV for under $100. Such a deal!

Do the Math

Budgeting your calories is similar to budgeting your money. Let's do the math. Studies show that the average person burns about 9 calories per pound of body weight each day just going through his or her regular motions. That would mean a 150-pound man would burn about 1,350 calories each day. A regular day includes getting dressed, working, shopping, running errands, and so on. If our 150-pound man consumed 1,350 calories each day, his weight would not change. If he chooses to eat more than 1,350 calories each day, he will have to burn them off through exercise or he will gain weight. If this man consumes 1,350 calories each day and exercises, he will lose weight. If he consumes less than 1,350 calories and exercises, he will lose weight more quickly.

As you can see, this is very much a math game, but this is where the strategy comes in. If you consumed only 1,200 calories worth of donuts each day and nothing else, you would lose weight. However, you would be hungry, tired, malnourished, and miserable. If you consumed only 1,200 calories each day based on the recipes in this book, you would be nourished, energetic, and satisfied. The moral of this story is spend your calories wisely.

Keep a Food Diary

An ideal way to manage your caloric intake and become more creative with your food choices is to keep a food diary. Most people tend to drastically underestimate the amount of calories they consume each day, which leads to confusion and frustration. Each recipe included here provides nutritional content to help you through this process. If you stray from this book, look up the nutritional information for those other foods. As you document your day, don't leave one bite or sip out, because it all counts. If you smear jelly on your breakfast toast, write it down. If you grab a jellybean out of your coworker's candy bowl, write it down. Even your beverages count. Document it all precisely and you'll learn where you are going right, where you are going wrong, and how you should move forward. Calorie management is one way to begin taking control over your layer of belly fat.

Foods to Be Wary Of

You'll notice this book contains starchy carbohydrates like pancakes and bread for breakfast and lunch but not much for dinner. Carbohydrates are designed to fuel your body. Eat them early to give yourself energy to get through your day. You do not need energy to sleep. Plus, starchy carbs like bread, pasta, and rice provide a lot less caloric bang for your buck than lean meats and veggies.

The dessert section is loaded with smoothies. Smoothies should not be considered a postworkout treat. It's a foolish mistake to burn a bunch of calories during a great workout and then consume an equal or greater amount when you're finished. Smoothies should be treated as a dessert. Choosing them over a hot fudge sundae is a wise choice, but be warned. They do not have some sort of magic power over weight loss. Stick to water while you work out and your benefits will not be lost.

You can still enjoy the simple pleasure of a PB&J, but stay away from white bread and sugary jellies. White bread is high on the glycemic index and doesn't do much for your health. Regular jelly and preserves are loaded with sugar! Cut your calories by 60 percent when you choose light-wheat bread and sugar-free preserves.

Last but not least, have fun! You don't need to obsess over food, you just have to get educated and start making consistently great choices about what you put in your mouth and what you do with your body. Be adventurous with the recipes you choose to try, and if you'd like to change them up a bit, go for it! Do you like Brussels sprouts more than bell peppers? Use them! Eating for a flat belly is not supposed to be hard. It is just a smarter way of eating, and you are one smart (fat-free) cookie!

Abdominal Muscles

Lean abdominals are amazing, and they have absolutely taken over as the status symbol of the day. Tight, firm abs are the most impressive commodity on the market at the moment, and it's about time you scored yourself a set. Ditching the belly fat has already been covered, and now it's time to put some effort into those muscles. You should start training them appropriately immediately, so when your layer of fat is long gone your abs will be ready for the spotlight.

Anatomy 101

The abdominals are comprised of the rectus abdominus, the obliques, and the transverse abdominus. The rectus abdominus runs from your rib cage past your belly button, down into your pubic crest. This muscle can be contracted by bringing your hips closer to your rib cage, as you do in regular crunches. The external and internal obliques run in a more diagonal pattern and are located on each side of the rectus abdominus. The obliques are responsible for trunk rotation (twisting) and lateral bending. The transverse abdominus is the deepest abdominal muscle. It is commonly referenced as a stabilizing belt for your trunk and spine. This muscle is not responsible for movement, but it is a vital component to lower back health. These muscles combine with those of the lower back to form what is commonly referred to as the core.

Work That Body!

Think about all of the ancient Roman statues you've seen. The men back then were ripped! It's probably fair to assume they didn't spend a lot of time doing crunches on a BOSU, so what was it that gave them all six packs? It was their life! They were manual laborers who lifted, pulled, and twisted against great resistance all day. They weren't surrounded by burger joints either, which certainly helps.

FACT

You may be surprised, but you are constantly working your abdominals. You use them throughout each day by simply executing great posture (suck in that transverse), shutting a door (rotate those obliques), and smooshing garbage down in to your trash can (flex that rectus)! As you rotate, bend, lift, and pull each day, your abdominal muscles are there to help.

In addition to helping you get through your day, some cardiovascular exercises can help you work your abs. Activities like martial arts, dancing, soccer, gymnastics, swimming, boxing, and basketball all require you to engage your core regularly. All of these options force you to twist and bend at the waist a lot, which is great work for your abdominals. The elliptical machine and the stationary bicycle do not. When you plan out your cardiovascular exercise, think about pursuing choices that will naturally work your core.

Abdominal Exercises

Abdominal work is a must! Firm abdominals are going to make you feel like a star. Just like your efforts with food, this a time for you to be strategic and consistent with your training.

Beyond Crunches

The abdominal exercises in this book are some of the most effective and efficient techniques you'll find. You don't have to do them all each day, but you do have to do them often. You should pursue abdominal strength training exercises for 5 to 20 minutes every other day. Your mission is to choose a variety of exercises that work each abdominal muscle in a challenging way. Start slowly and progress to extremely challenging exercises. How will you know if a certain exercise is extremely challenging? Give it a try and you'll find out. The exercises that you cannot already do will be the ones you should strive to accomplish.

Do not spend 20 minutes lying on your back doing 500 crunches. That would be an insane waste of your time. In fact, when it comes to strength training, if you can do more than 20 repetitions of one exercise it is too easy for you. At that point, it's time for you to increase the level of difficulty or resistance.

Here are some basic rules to live by:

- Train your abdominals between 5 and 20 minutes every other day.
- Perform at least five different exercises each time you train.
- If you can do more than 20 repetitions of one exercise, increase the level of difficulty.
- Spend an equal amount of time training your rectus and your obliques.
- To maintain balance, spend at least 5 minutes every other day training the muscles of your lower back.

The following exercises will help you get your abs into shape. Begin with sets of 5 to 20. If five is hard for you, do five. If twenty becomes too easy, increase the level of difficulty or try a more challenging exercise.

Small Ball Rotational Crunch

1. With knees bent and chin up, rest at the top of a crunch with your back just touching a 6" rubber ball.
2. Rotate to your right, touching the right elbow to the ground and looking at the floor.
3. Immediately contract and return to starting position.
4. Rotate to the right 10 times in a row, and then perform 10 repetitions on the left side.

Straight Leg Stretch with Small Ball

1. Lie face up on the ground, bend your left knee and extend your right leg with pointed toe. Hold a 6" ball in your hands with your arms extended over your head.
2. Keeping your elbows straight, bring the ball up toward the ceiling as you raise your right leg off the ground. Your arms should be straight out in front of you, and your heel should be 6 to 10 inches off the ground.
3. Return to first position and repeat 10 times before switching legs.

Full Knee to Shoulder Crunch with Small Ball

1. Lie face-up with your hands supporting your elevated head, elbows wide and legs perpendicular to the floor with a 6" ball between your feet. Make sure your legs extend long and your toes are pointed.
2. Simultaneously lift your shoulders and hips toward the ceiling and then lower your legs as far toward the ground as you can without back pain. Maintain long legs throughout the entire movement. Return to starting position and repeat.

Windmill

1. Lie face-up with your legs extended perpendicular to the floor with a 6" ball in between your feet and arms out at your sides, palms down.
2. Slowly lower your legs to left, trying to keep as much of your back on the floor as possible. Slowly return to the middle and then go to the right. Repeat.

Long Leg Switch

1. Lie face-up with both shoulders and feet elevated slightly off the floor, legs extended and toes pointed.
2. Lift your right leg toward the ceiling, gently clasp it with your hands, and contract shoulders toward right thigh.
3. Bring the right leg down as your left leg rises, gently clasp it with your hands, and contract shoulders toward left thigh.

Swiss Ball Crunch

1. Lie face-up with your mid back on the Swiss ball and your feet flat on the ground.
2. Extend your shoulders as far back as you can (keep your chin toward the ceiling), and then contract your abs to lift your shoulders toward the ceiling.

Swiss Ball Rotational Crunch

1. Lie face-up with your mid back on the Swiss ball and your feet flat on the ground.
2. Extend your shoulders as far back as you can (keep your chin toward the ceiling), and rotate and lift your left shoulder up to the ceiling and across your body.
3. Repeat with your right shoulder and continue to alternate sides throughout the set.

Traditional Oblique Crunch

1. Lie flat on your back with your hands supporting your head, elbows wide and knees bent and resting to the left.
2. Lift your shoulders toward the ceiling by contracting your abdominals and return to the ground.
3. Do 10 or more repetitions on this side and repeat with your knees resting on your right side.

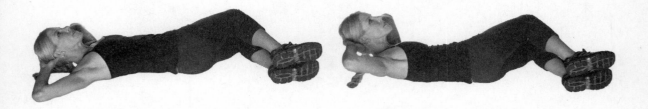

Pike

1. Use mats or a Roman chair to elevate your body onto your hands. Lift both legs straight out in front of you parallel to the ground and hold as long as you can.
2. Rest and repeat.

V Sit

1. Balance on your bottom and elevate both legs at a 45° angle toward the ceiling. Keep your legs and back as straight as possible. Reach your arms in the same direction as your feet or hold them high above your head. Hold this position as long as you can maintain proper form. Beginners should aim for 5 seconds. Advanced folks should aim for 30 to 60 seconds.
2. Rest and repeat.

BOSU Rock

1. Assume full pushup position (flat back, legs and arms extended) with hands on the flat side of the BOSU balance tool.
2. Maintain this stiff posture and press your right knuckles toward the ground while pressing down on the BOSU.
3. Slowly rise to center and press your left knuckles down toward the ground.
4. Repeat this as many times as you can while maintaining a flat back and proper form.

Chapter 2
Rise and Shine, It's Breakfast Time!

Basic Scrambled Eggs

Serves 1

50 calories
0g fat
2g carbohydrates
10g protein
170mg sodium
0g fiber

Ingredients
½ cup Egg Beaters
Dash of salt and pepper

Keep a container of Egg Beaters or a similar egg substitute in your refrigerator and make use of it when you hit the snooze button too many times.

1. Pour Egg Beaters into a microwave-safe bowl. Add salt and pepper to taste. Heat in microwave for 45 seconds.

2. Stir eggs and heat in microwave on high for additional 20 seconds.

3. Repeat step two until eggs are desired consistency.

Food Is Fuel
Consume your largest meal in the morning and decrease the size of each meal throughout the day. You wouldn't take a long car trip with your gas tank on empty and fill up once you arrived at your destination. Your body needs fuel to go, so feed it at the beginning of your day.

Meaty Scrambled Eggs

Vary the types of lean turkey or other meats you use in these eggs. Try it with leftovers from the night before.

1. Pour all the ingredients into a microwave-safe bowl.
2. Follow directions for Basic Scrambled Eggs (page 16).

Serves 1

81 calories
0g fat
2g carbohydrates
16g protein
576mg sodium
0g fiber

Ingredients
½ cup Egg Beaters
Dash of salt and pepper
1 slice low-sodium deli turkey, chopped

Festive Scrambled Eggs

A quarter cup of Egg Beaters is the equivalent of one egg. Do the math with your recipes that ask for real eggs and make the substitution to save yourself tons of fat!

1. Pour all ingredients into a microwave-safe bowl.
2. Follow directions for Basic Scrambled Eggs (page 16).

Serves 1

97 calories
1g fat
4g carbohydrates
16g protein
437mg sodium
0g fiber

Ingredients
½ cup Egg Beaters
Dash of salt and pepper
1 slice 95 percent fat-free turkey bacon, cooked and chopped
2 tablespoons tomatoes, diced
1 tablespoon bell peppers, diced

Pilates

Pilates is a superb form of exercise if you're striving for a strong core. The practice focuses on the deep and lateral transverse abdominal muscle. Pilates combines stretching and strengthening exercises that target the abdominals, gluteals, and lower back muscles. It can benefit elite athletes, those recovering from injuries, and everyone in between.

Basic Breakfast Sandwich

Serves 1

180 calories
1g fat
27g carbohydrates
22g protein
680mg sodium
8g fiber

Ingredients
1 light-wheat English muffin
½ cup Egg Beaters
Dash of salt and pepper
1 slice fat-free American cheese

Light English muffins are almost always going to be your best choice when it comes to breads at breakfast. They're significantly lower in calories than bagels and regular white bread.

1. Toast English muffin halves.

2. Pour eggs, salt, and pepper into a microwave-safe bowl.

3. Microwave egg mixture for 1 minute on high or until egg is thoroughly cooked.

4. Place eggs on one side of the toasted muffin, add cheese, and top with the other half of the muffin.

Italian Breakfast Sandwich

Serves 1

317 calories
1g fat
29g carbohydrates
53g protein
1,273mg sodium
8g fiber

Ingredients
1 light-wheat English muffin
½ cup Egg Beaters
Dash of salt and pepper
2 tablespoons tomatoes, diced
1/8 teaspoon basil
1 slice fat-free mozzarella cheese

Egg Beaters is the most popular brand of fat-free egg substitute, but you can shop generic egg substitutes as well. Money matters, and most of these products are indistinguishable.

1. Toast English muffin halves.

2. Mix eggs, salt, pepper, tomatoes, and basil in a microwave-safe bowl.

3. Microwave egg mixture for 1 minute on high or until egg mixture is thoroughly cooked.

4. Place egg mixture on one side of the toasted muffin, add cheese, and top with the other half of the muffin.

Western Breakfast Sandwich

Canadian bacon is far leaner than regular bacon. Regular bacon contains about 120 calories and 9 grams of fat per ounce, and Canadian bacon contains about 34 calories and 1 gram of fat per ounce.

1. Toast English muffin halves.

2. Mix eggs, salt, pepper, tomatoes, peppers, and onions in a microwave-safe bowl.

3. Microwave egg mixture for 1 minute on high or until egg is thoroughly cooked.

4. Place egg mixture on one side of the toasted muffin, add cheese and bacon, and top with the other half of the muffin.

Serves 1

236 calories
3g fat
30g carbohydrates
28g protein
1,082mg sodium
9g fiber

Ingredients
1 light-wheat English muffin
½ cup Egg Beaters
Dash of salt and pepper
2 tablespoons tomatoes, diced
1 tablespoon bell peppers, diced
1 tablespoon onions, diced
1 slice fat-free American cheese
1 slice Canadian bacon, cooked

Mexican Breakfast Sandwich

Serves 1

171 calories
2g fat
26g carbohydrates
19g protein
564mg sodium
9g fiber

Ingredients
1 light-wheat English muffin
½ cup Egg Beaters
Dash of salt and pepper
1 tablespoon shredded fat-
    free Cheddar cheese
2 tablespoons salsa

To add even more flavor to this recipe, chop up some onions and peppers and throw them into the bowl before cooking your eggs.

1. Toast English muffin halves.

2. Mix eggs, salt, pepper, and cheese in a microwave-safe bowl.

3. Microwave egg mixture for 1 minute on high or until egg is thoroughly cooked.

4. Place egg mixture on one side of the toasted muffin, add salsa, and top with the other half of the muffin.

Exercise Is Deliberate

There is a difference between being active and exercising. Housework and playing at the park with the kids are examples of being active. Exercise should require you to huff, puff, grunt, and wince. Challenging yourself is how you make progress. If you set aside deliberate time for legitimate exercise and work hard, your body will respond accordingly.

Protein and Berry Pita

When deciding which berries to use in this recipe, test out a variety. In fact, it's always a good idea to give preferential treatment to in-season produce.

1. In a small bowl mix: ricotta, vanilla and Splenda.

2. Add berries to ricotta mix.

3. Open pita and scoop ricotta mix into middle.

How Often Should You Exercise?

With 168 hours in each week, it really isn't such an irrational suggestion for you to engage in 6 to 8 hours of deliberate exercise per week. Because of the time spent sleeping, eating, driving, watching television, and sitting at a desk working, most people lead fairly sedentary lives. Exercise vigorously most days of the week and you'll be more likely to achieve your physical goals.

Serves 1

133 calories
1g fat
23g carbohydrates
10g protein
261mg sodium
3g fiber

Ingredients
3 tablespoons fat-free ricotta cheese
½ teaspoon vanilla extract
½ teaspoon Splenda
3 tablespoons your favorite berries
½ whole wheat pita

Protein and Peaches Pita

If the canned peaches seem a little too juicy for you,
use a fresh diced peach instead.

In a small bowl mix ricotta, vanilla, and Splenda. Add diced peaches to the ricotta mix. Open the pita and scoop ricotta mix into the middle.

Serves 1

179 calories
1g fat
36g carbohydrates
9g protein
288mg sodium
4g fiber

Ingredients

3 tablespoons fat-free ricotta cheese
½ teaspoon vanilla extract
½ teaspoon Splenda
4-ounce cup no-sugar-added diced peaches
½ whole wheat pita

Crunchy Creamy Yogurt Parfait

Yogurt parfaits are traditionally a healthy choice.
If you are going to order one while you're out, first confirm that the yogurt is
low-fat and avoid the caloric granola topping.

Layer the ingredients in a tall cup, starting with the bran flakes, then the yogurt, and finally the strawberries.

Serves 1

210 calories
1g fat
46g carbohydrates
9g protein
295mg sodium
6g fiber

Ingredients

2 tablespoons bran flakes cereal
4 ounces sugar-free vanilla yogurt
¼ cup sliced strawberries

Herbed Cheese Omelet

Chives provide a mild onionlike flavor.
They make a great addition to eggs, potatoes, and fish.
Add chives to hot food last because heat tends to lessen their flavor.

1. Combine cream cheese and chives in a small bowl.

2. In another bowl, combine eggs, water, salt, and pepper.

3. Coat a skillet with nonstick spray. Pour the eggs into the skillet and cook on medium heat until the edges start to set (less than a minute).

4. Tilt the pan so uncooked egg moves beneath the cooked portion. Continue to cook and tilt until the center of the eggs is no longer runny.

5. Place cream cheese mix on half of the eggs and fold the second half over. Lift the pan up by the handle and slide the omelet onto a plate.

Serves 1

70 calories
0g fat
4g carbohydrates
14g protein
323mg sodium
0g fiber

Ingredients

2 tablespoons fat-free cream cheese
1 tablespoon chopped chives
½ cup Egg Beaters
1 teaspoon water
Pinch salt
Pinch pepper

Prosciutto and Sun-Dried Tomato Strata

Serves 1

321 calories
8g fat
37g carbohydrates
29g protein
1,730mg sodium
7g fiber

Ingredients

½ cup fat-free milk
1 tablespoon fat-free sour
    cream
¼ cup Egg Beaters
1 tablespoon sun-dried
    tomatoes, chopped
1/8 teaspoon fresh garlic,
    minced
2 slices toasted whole wheat
    bread, cubed
1 ounce prosciutto, chopped
1 tablespoon shredded fat-
    free mozzarella cheese
1 tablespoon grated reduced-
    fat Parmesan cheese

*To save time in the morning, assemble all of the ingredients
the night before and chill them in the refrigerator overnight.
Bake in the morning for a quick, lean breakfast.*

1. In a large bowl, mix milk, sour cream, and Egg Beaters. Add tomatoes and garlic and blend well. Add bread cubes, stirring gently.

2. Spray two or three muffin molds in a muffin pan with nonstick spray. Scoop 2 tablespoons of strata mixture into the bottom of each muffin mold.

3. Divide prosciutto, mozzarella, and Parmesan between all the molds. Top with remaining strata mixture.

4. Bake uncovered at 350°F for 15 to 20 minutes or until egg is thoroughly cooked.

Mexican Omelet

*To make this a more muscular Mexican omelet,
add 2 tablespoons of black beans for added protein.*

1. Coat a skillet with nonstick spray. Add Egg Beaters to skillet and salt and pepper to taste. Cook on medium high for 3 minutes.

2. Flip eggs and add salsa and cheese to the center of the eggs. Fold omelet over and cook for another 2 minutes, then flip and cook for an additional 2 minutes.

Financial Frustrations with Food

A common myth is that eating healthy is far more expensive than eating garbage. A pound of bananas cost about $0.60 while a pound of crackers can cost around $4.00! Where else can you find an entire pound of food for less than a dollar in any place other than the produce section? Save money and eat healthy.

Serves 1

75 calories
0g fat
4g carbohydrates
14g protein
428mg sodium
1g fiber

Ingredients
¼ cup Egg Beaters
Salt and pepper to taste
2 tablespoons salsa
1 slice fat-free Cheddar
   cheese

Greek Omelet

This recipe would not work very well with frozen spinach. Although frozen spinach is very convenient, it would require too much time to defrost.

Serves 1

55 calories
2g fat
2g carbohydrates
7g protein
202mg sodium
1g fiber

Ingredients

¼ cup Egg Beaters
Salt and pepper to taste
½ cup fresh spinach, chopped
1 tablespoon tomatoes, diced
1 tablespoon feta cheese,
    crumbled

1. Coat a skillet with nonstick spray. Add Egg Beaters to skillet and salt and pepper to taste. Cook on medium high for 3 minutes.

2. Flip eggs and add spinach, tomatoes, and cheese to the center of the eggs. Fold omelet over and cook for another 2 minutes, then flip and cook for an additional 2 minutes.

Western Frittata

When shopping for deli meat, check out the nutritional information and seek out meats that are low in sodium.

Serves 1

87 calories
0g fat
7g carbohydrates
15g protein
632mg sodium
0g fiber

Ingredients

1 tablespoon white onions,
    chopped
1 tablespoon bell peppers,
    chopped
1 ounce lean low-sodium deli
    ham or turkey, cubed
¼ cup Egg Beaters
1 slice fat-free American
    cheese

1. Coat a skillet with nonstick spray. On medium-high heat, add onions, peppers, and ham to skillet. Sauté for 2 minutes.

2. Add Egg Beaters to skillet and cook for 2 to 3 minutes. Place cheese on top of frittata, then place skillet in oven under the broiler and broil for 2 to 3 minutes or until cheese melts and eggs are set. Remove from pan and serve.

Mushroom and Turkey Bacon Frittata

Turkey bacon is significantly lower in trans fats and calories than regular bacon. Minor details like this will slowly drive you toward healthier habits and a leaner body.

1. Coat a skillet with nonstick spray. Add onions, mushrooms, and turkey bacon to the skillet and sauté for 2 minutes over medium-high heat.

2. Add Egg Beaters to skillet and cook for 2 to 3 minutes, then place skillet in oven under the broiler and broil for 2 to 3 minutes or until eggs are set.

Food Is for Fuel, Not Fun
Food can be incredibly enjoyable, but don't forget that its main purpose is to keep you alive and kicking. Since fitness is a priority for you, make an effort to schedule fun activities that don't revolve around food. Make plans to play sports, go dancing, or see a show.

Serves 1

72 calories
1g fat
3g carbohydrates
11g protein
362mg sodium
0g fiber

Ingredients
2 tablespoons white onions, sliced
2 tablespoons white mushrooms, sliced
2 tablespoons 95 percent fat-free turkey bacon, chopped
¼ cup Egg Beaters

California Omelet

To cook asparagus, add asparagus to 2 cups of boiling water and cook for 3 minutes. Remove asparagus and immediately soak in cold water for 5 minutes.

1. Coat a skillet with nonstick spray. Add Egg Beaters to skillet and salt and pepper to taste. Cook on medium high for 3 minutes.

2. Flip omelet and add asparagus, cheese, and red peppers to the center of the eggs. Fold omelet over and cook for 2 minutes, then flip and cook for an additional 2 minutes.

Wobble for Washboard Abs
A smart way to get some extra ab work is to utilize a balance tool like the BOSU while training other body parts. Instead of doing bicep curls on the ground, try doing them while standing on a BOSU. The instability involved in standing on this wobbly tool requires your core to constantly contract to keep you stable.

Serves 1

84 calories
0g fat
10g carbohydrates
12g protein
393mg sodium
2g fiber

Ingredients
¼ cup Egg Beaters
Salt and pepper to taste
¼ cup asparagus spears, cooked and cut
1 slice fat-free white American cheese
2 tablespoons roasted red peppers, chopped

Veggie Omelet

You can get really creative with omelets. Make a list of your favorite veggies and spend a few days trying them out in omelets.

1. Coat a skillet with nonstick spray. Sauté broccoli, onions, and mushrooms for 4 minutes over medium-high heat.

2. Remove veggies from skillet and place in a bowl with tomatoes. Add Egg Beaters to skillet and cook on medium high for 2 minutes on each side.

3. Add vegetable mixture to middle of omelet and fold over. Serve immediately.

Training with a Partner
Accomplishing a fitness-oriented goal is often more easily attained and enjoyable if it is done with a partner. It's harder to miss a workout if a partner is expecting you, and you're likely to work harder with a pal. You're also more likely to enjoy your workouts with a friend.

Serves 1

77 calories
1g fat
12g carbohydrates
8g protein
100mg sodium
3g fiber

Ingredients
¼ cup broccoli, chopped
2 tablespoons white onions, sliced
2 tablespoons white mushrooms, sliced
2 tablespoons tomatoes, diced
¼ cup Egg Beaters

Tropical Muffins

Healthy muffins are fine for breakfast as long as you stick to eating only one. To fight off hunger early in the day, enjoy them with a high-protein dish like eggs.

1. Mix flour and Splenda and make a well in the center.

2. In a separate bowl, combine coconut milk, Smart Squeeze, lemon rind, vanilla extract, and Egg Beaters. Mix well with a whisk.

3. Add liquid mixture to flour mixture. Stir until moist. Add tropical fruit and fold into mixture. Spray a medium-size muffin pan with nonstick spray.

4. Spoon batter into muffin molds. Bake at 400°F for 20 minutes or until a toothpick inserted into the center of a muffin comes out dry.

Breakfast Salad

Mandarin oranges are a citrus fruit that really look more flat like a tangerine than round like an orange. High in vitamin C, you should always choose canned mandarin oranges without the heavy syrup.

Combine all ingredients in a large bowl and serve.

Peach Salad with Mint Dressing

The blueberries and raspberries in this recipe provide high levels of antioxidants, which are powerful cancer-fighting tools.

1. Thoroughly wash all fresh fruit and cucumber.

2. Once dry, combine in a large bowl.

3. Mix dressing ingredients in a separate bowl.

4. Gently toss dressing with fruit mixture and serve immediately.

Should You Hire a Personal Trainer?
Personal trainers function in several ways. They teach you new ways to exercise, educate you about your body, push you to work harder, and serve as motivation to stick to your schedule. If you need support in any of these areas, maybe you should give a personal trainer a try!

Serves 4

66 calories
0g fat
17g carbohydrates
1g protein
268mg sodium
3g fiber

Ingredients
2 cups fresh peaches, sliced
1 cup cucumber, peeled, seeded, and thinly sliced
½ cup fresh raspberries
¼ cup fresh blueberries
½ teaspoon lemon rind, grated
1 tablespoon fresh lemon juice
2 teaspoons fresh mint, minced
2 teaspoons honey
½ teaspoon salt
¼ teaspoon black pepper

Basic Whole Wheat Pancakes

*Add blueberries, bananas and pecans, cranberries and walnuts,
or cinnamon and raisins to the batter before you cook the pancakes.
Come up with fun toppings of your own.*

Serves 6

64 calories
0g fat
12g carbohydrates
4g protein
141mg sodium
2g fiber

Ingredients
½ cup whole wheat flour
¼ cup quick-cooking oatmeal
1 tablespoon Splenda
½ teaspoon baking powder
1/3 teaspoon baking soda
1/8 cup egg white substitute
1 cup skim milk

1. In a bowl, mix all dry ingredients together. In a separate bowl, mix all wet ingredients together. Gently fold dry ingredients into wet ingredients.

2. Coat skillet or griddle with nonstick spray. Pour ⅓ cup batter per pancake onto skillet.

3. Cook on medium-high heat until pancake develops bubbles on top. Flip the pancake and brown on the other side.

Fat Facts
According to U.S. government regulations, food containing less than 0.5 grams of fat per serving is called fat-free. Three grams of fat or less per serving earns the title low-fat. And food containing at least 25 percent less fat than the original version of the food is identified as reduced fat.

Pumpkin and White Chocolate Whole Wheat Pancakes

Using tiny bits of something indulgent like chocolate once in a while is a sneaky way to jazz up a really healthy dish.

1. In a bowl, mix all dry ingredients together. In a separate bowl, mix all wet ingredients together. Gently fold dry ingredients into wet ingredients.

2. Coat skillet or griddle with nonstick spray. Pour ⅓ cup batter per pancake onto skillet.

3. Cook on medium-high heat until pancake develops bubbles on top. Flip the pancake and brown on the other side.

All or Nothing?
Eating healthy is not an all-or-nothing activity. Make the majority of your food choices great. If 90 percent of your meals are full of lean protein, produce, lean dairy, and whole grains, indulging in less than nutritious choices 10 percent of the time won't hurt you so much.

Serves 6

100 calories
2g fat
17g carbohydrates
4g protein
148mg sodium
2g fiber

Ingredients
½ cup whole wheat flour
¼ cup quick-cooking oatmeal
1 tablespoon Splenda
½ teaspoon baking powder
1/3 teaspoon baking soda
1/8 cup egg white substitute
1 cup skim milk
1½ cups canned pumpkin
½ teaspoon ground
    cinnamon
1 teaspoon Splenda brown
    sugar
2 tablespoons white
    chocolate morsels

Apple Pie Whole Wheat Pancakes

Serves 6

87 calories
1g fat
17g carbohydrates
4g protein
141mg sodium
2g fiber

Ingredients

½ cup whole wheat flour
¼ cup quick-cooking oatmeal
1 tablespoon Splenda
½ teaspoon baking powder
1/3 teaspoon baking soda
1/8 cup egg white substitute
1 cup skim milk
1½ cups Gala apples, sliced
½ teaspoon cinnamon
1/8 teaspoon nutmeg

Enjoy the taste of dessert without all of the fat and calories that come with it. To get the flavor of apple pie a la mode, serve these pancakes with ½ cup of fat-free vanilla yogurt.

1. In a bowl, mix all dry ingredients together. In a separate bowl, mix all wet ingredients together. Gently fold dry ingredients into wet ingredients.

2. Coat skillet or griddle with nonstick spray. Pour ⅓ cup batter per pancake onto skillet.

3. Cook on medium-high heat until pancake develops bubbles on top. Flip the pancake and brown on the other side.

Monster of the Morning

Did you know that 1 cup of traditional maple syrup used on pancakes packs a whopping 800 calories? Even if you used one-fourth that much, it's still a monster amount to consume. Hold to high standards in the morning and insist on using a sugar-free version of maple syrup, which only packs 122 calories per cup, whenever the opportunity arises.

Sweet Potato Pie Pancakes

Serve this dish in early November to get your family ready for and excited about Thanksgiving dinner or a fall harvest celebration.

1. In a bowl, mix all dry ingredients together. In a separate bowl, mix all wet ingredients together. Gently fold dry ingredients into wet ingredients.

2. Coat skillet or griddle with nonstick spray. Pour ⅓ cup batter per pancake onto skillet.

3. Cook on medium-high heat until pancake develops bubbles on top. Flip the pancake and brown on the other side.

Serves 6

122 calories
1g fat
26g carbohydrates
4g protein
160mg sodium
3g fiber

Ingredients
½ cup whole wheat flour
¼ cup quick-cooking oatmeal
1 tablespoon Splenda
½ teaspoon baking powder
1/3 teaspoon baking soda
1/8 cup egg white substitute
1 cup skim milk
1½ cups canned sweet
    potatoes
2 tablespoons pecans,
    chopped
½ teaspoon cinnamon
1 teaspoon Splenda brown
    sugar
½ teaspoon vanilla extract

Fun and Fruity Pancakes

Serves 6

114 calories
1g fat
25g carbohydrates
5g protein
143mg sodium
4g fiber

Ingredients
½ cup whole wheat flour
¼ cup quick-cooking oatmeal
1 tablespoon Splenda
½ teaspoon baking powder
1/3 teaspoon baking soda
1/8 cup egg white substitute
1 cup skim milk
2 cups peaches, peeled and
    sliced
¾ teaspoon cinnamon
1 banana, sliced
1 tablespoon fresh lemon
    juice
1 cup strawberries, sliced
1 cup seedless grapes

If you'd like to save some time and energy, grab two 8-ounce cans of sliced peaches instead of using fresh ones. Just make sure you choose peaches in their own juice, not in syrup.

1. In a bowl, mix all dry ingredients together. In a separate bowl, mix egg substitute and milk. Gently fold dry ingredients into wet ingredients.

2. Coat skillet or griddle with nonstick spray. Pour ⅓ cup batter per pancake onto skillet.

3. Cook on medium-high heat until pancake develops bubbles on top. Flip the pancake and brown on the other side.

4. In a separate bowl, toss peach slices with cinnamon. Wet banana with lemon juice and add to the bowl. Toss strawberries, grapes, and bananas in the bowl with the peaches. Evenly top cooked pancakes with fruit mixture.

Banana Trick
A simple way to prevent peeled bananas from browning is to moisten them with lemon juice. This will not affect the taste in any way; it will just keep them fresh and firm the way you would want them to be. Unsweetened pineapple juice serves this purpose as well.

Hawaiian Pancakes

Serve these pancakes with freshly cut pineapple chunks before a day at the beach to get yourself in the mood.

Follow the Basic Whole Wheat Pancakes recipe directions (page 32). Prior to cooking, add pineapple and coconut to batter.

Banish the Bagel?
Bagels traditionally pack between 200 and 500 calories each. Ideally you'll avoid them, but if you're going to have one, make it whole wheat, scoop out the bready guts, and fill the crust with protein or veggies. A better choice would be a light-wheat English muffin.

Serves 6

96 calories
1g fat
19g carbohydrates
4g protein
145mg sodium
2g fiber

Ingredients
½ cup whole wheat flour
¼ cup quick-cooking oatmeal
1 tablespoon Splenda
½ teaspoon baking powder
1/3 teaspoon baking soda
1/8 cup egg white substitute
1 cup skim milk
1 cup canned crushed
    pineapples, drained
2 tablespoons shredded
    coconut flakes

French Toast

Quite often, people sprinkle powdered sugar on their French toast to add a bit of sweetness. Since you're on a mission to whittle your middle, skip the sugar and sweeten with sugar-free maple syrup instead.

1. Coat a skillet with nonstick spray. Mix Egg Beaters, Splenda, vanilla, and cinnamon in a bowl. Dip and coat each slice of bread in egg mixture.

2. Cook bread on each side in skillet on medium high until it begins to brown.

Serves 4

72 calories
1g fat
13g carbohydrates
7g protein
203mg sodium
3g fiber

Ingredients
1 cup Egg Beaters
2 teaspoons Splenda
½ teaspoon vanilla
¼ teaspoon cinnamon
4 slices light-wheat bread

California English Muffin

Food referenced as "California" style is traditionally fresh, uncomplicated cuisine that makes the most of locally grown ingredients.

Split and toast English muffin. Spread 1 tablespoon cream cheese on each English muffin half. Top each half with 1 slice of tomato and sprouts. Salt and pepper to taste.

Satiety
People tend to enjoy the feeling of satiety and rarely stop the act of consumption until they've achieved it. This is why it's crucial not to drink your calories. One could drink 1,500 calories of beer, soda, or juice and never feel full! Drink calorie-free beverages and get your calories from actual food.

Chapter 3
Lunch Break

Oven "Fried" Southern Chicken

Serves 6

181 calories
2g fat
9g carbohydrates
29g protein
200mg sodium
0g fiber

Ingredients

1 cup buttermilk
½ teaspoon all-purpose
    seasoning
½ teaspoon hot sauce
½ teaspoon fresh garlic,
    minced
½ teaspoon olive oil
6 boneless, skinless chicken
    breasts
1 cup corn flakes, crushed
3 tablespoons flour

Instead of giving in to the enticing aroma of fried chicken oozing out of the deli in your grocery store, race home and whip up this recipe instead. It provides a genuinely crispy flavor without leaving you with a greasy chin.

1. Coat cookie sheet with cooking spray and set aside.

2. Mix buttermilk, all-purpose seasoning, hot sauce, garlic, olive oil, and chicken breasts.

3. Crush corn flakes and mix with flour in a separate bowl.

4. Take each chicken breast from the milk mixture and coat with dry mixture. Place chicken on the cookie sheet.

5. Bake uncovered at 370°F for 35 to 40 minutes.

Italian Turkey Burgers

To save a ton of useless calories and still have a casing for your burger, try substituting slightly grilled portabella mushrooms for traditional burger buns.

1. Mix all ingredients except burgers. Coat a 9" × 13" baking dish with nonstick spray. Lay turkey burgers in dish without overlapping.

2. Pour mixture over burgers and cover with foil. Bake at 375°F for 25 minutes.

Spousal Stumbling Blocks
Of course, you'd love for your honey to achieve great health, but don't use his or her poor habits as an excuse to hold you back. Instead, take control over your own life and make fitness a habit. As you become more successful, your partner might just jump on board. But really, only you are responsible for you!

Serves 6

232 calories
13g fat
4g carbohydrates
25g protein
302mg sodium
1g fiber

Ingredients
1 tablespoon olive oil
1 clove fresh garlic, minced
½ teaspoon all-purpose
   seasoning
1 cup marinara sauce
¼ cup white onions, chopped
1 tablespoon fresh parsley
½ cup shredded fat-free
   mozzarella cheese
6 lean turkey burgers

Ingredients

1 small whole wheat tortilla
½ serving Simply Grilled
   Chicken Breasts (page
   176), cooked
1 tablespoon shredded low-
   fat Cheddar cheese
½ tablespoon plum
   tomatoes, diced
½ tablespoon red onion,
   diced
1 tablespoon black beans
½ tablespoon fat-free sour
   cream
½ tablespoon salsa

Fiesta Chicken Wrap

*Instead of using sour cream and salsa for this recipe, you could try a little sauce
made by mixing 1 cup fat-free ranch and 1 teaspoon chili powder.*

Lay tortilla flat on a plate. Slice chicken. Place all ingredients in the
center of the tortilla. Roll tortilla into a wrap.

Fast Food

*Many people use limited time as an excuse to eat poorly. Baloney! Healthy
food can be quick, and fast-food joints are bending over backward to
appease the health-conscious consumer. So go ahead and zoom through
that drive-thru. Just order lean meat and fresh or raw veggies; ignore
everything fried.*

Buffalo Chicken Wrap

*If you ever go to a sports bar and need to satisfy this craving,
order grilled chicken instead of deep-fried wings and dip
them into a small cup of wing sauce.*

1. Lay tortilla flat on a plate. Slice chicken and coat in wing sauce.
   Spread cream cheese on tortilla. Place coated chicken, Cheddar, lettuce, and tomatoes on tortilla.

2. Roll tortilla into a wrap. Serve with a celery stalk and dip wrap in
   ranch dressing to taste.

Pack a Picnic!

*Instead of relying on restaurant food or fast food for meals away from
home, pack a picnic. Throw a fresh salad, grilled lean meat, and fresh
fruit in a cooler and bring it to work with you. Getting some fresh air
while enjoying some truly fresh food is the perfect way to spend some
time on your health and mental well-being.*

Serves 1

245 calories
4g fat
30g carbohydrates
22g protein
622mg sodium
2g fiber

Ingredients

*1 small whole wheat tortilla
½ serving Simply Grilled
    Chicken Breasts (page
    176), cooked
1 teaspoon Crystal Wing
    Sauce
1 tablespoon fat-free cream
    cheese
1 tablespoon shredded low-
    fat Cheddar cheese
½ cup chopped romaine
    lettuce
1 tablespoon tomatoes, diced
1 celery stalk
½ tablespoon fat-free ranch
    dressing*

Turkey Walnut Wrap

The honey-roasted turkey slices create a sweet taste for this wrap, but feel free to try smoked turkey or any other sort of turkey breast that catches your eye.

Serves 1

280 calories
10g fat
32g carbohydrates
18g protein
1,164mg sodium
4g fiber

Ingredients

1 small whole wheat tortilla
2 deli slices of honey-roasted turkey breast
½ cup fresh spinach
1 teaspoon walnuts
1 tablespoon avocadoes, diced
2 tablespoons mushrooms, sliced
2 tablespoons sun-dried tomatoes, sliced
1 teaspoon crumbled blue cheese

Place tortilla flat on a plate. Place turkey flat on tortilla. Cover turkey with the remaining ingredients. Roll tortilla into a wrap.

Why Use a Swiss Ball?
A Swiss ball allows you a wide range of motion while you do your abdominal exercises. When you do crunches on the floor, the abs have limited extension potential. Since abdominals can extend into a bridge, the Swiss ball provides back support while allowing you to work through a full range of motion.

Tuna Burgers

If you're having a luau or a pool party, these burgers are a perfect choice for your tropical theme! Your friends will think you're so clever. Aloha!

1. In a medium bowl, combine ¾ cup bread crumbs and all other ingredients. Blend well. Divide into six burgers and top with remaining bread crumbs.

2. Coat a large skillet with nonstick spray. Place burgers in skillet and cook each side on medium heat for 3 to 5 minutes or until golden brown.

Beyond Basic Burgers

Burgers are a staple in the lives of millions of people around the world. They make appearances for lunch, dinner, and snacks. Unfortunately, traditional burgers can be a nightmare for your health and your waistline. Stick to your guns and make sure you only choose burgers made with lean meat. And while you're at it, ditch the buns altogether.

Serves 6

140 calories
2g fat
13g carbohydrates
16g protein
507mg sodium
0g fiber

Ingredients

1½ cups bread crumbs
10 ounces canned light tuna, in chunks
½ cup shredded fat-free Cheddar cheese
½ cup fat-free peppercorn dressing
¼ cup Egg Beaters
¼ cup green onion, sliced

Tuna Salad Pita

Make up a large batch of Mom's Tuna Salad once a week. It's a perfect addition to salads, sandwiches, and pitas.

Fill pita pocket with tuna, lettuce, and tomatoes.

Serves 1

227 calories
2g fat
28g carbohydrates
26g protein
848mg sodium
4g fiber

Ingredients
½ whole wheat pita
3 ounces Mom's Tuna Salad (page 258)
½ cup romaine lettuce, chopped
¼ cup plum tomato, diced

Spankin' Good News!
You are on a mission to remove belly fat and harden up the muscles of your abdominals. If you're a woman and you're not exactly where you want to be yet, invest in Spanx! Spanx makes sturdy undergarments that help flatten, smooth things out, and suck things in.

All-American Burger Bowl

This recipe offers all the tasty flavor of a traditional beef burger without most of the fat. Serving it up in a bowl instead of on a bun will save you at least 200 calories.

Serves 1

187 calories
7g fat
10g carbohydrates
19g protein
1,222 mg sodium
3g fiber

Ingredients
3 ounces 90 percent lean ground turkey
2 tablespoons yellow onion, diced
¼ cup tomato, diced
½ cup romaine lettuce, chopped
1 teaspoon low sodium ketchup
1 teaspoon yellow mustard
1 small dill pickle

1. In a small skillet, grill turkey for 6 minutes on medium heat. Add onions to skillet and grill for another 3 minutes.

2. Put turkey, onions, tomatoes, and lettuce in a small bowl and mix. Add ketchup and mustard to taste. Enjoy with a pickle on the side.

Italian Burger Bowl

*To increase the nutritional value of this recipe,
choose a marinara sauce full of chunky vegetables.*

Place ground veggie burger in a bowl; microwave for 1 minute. Add ricotta and marinara to burger; stir. Heat for another 30 seconds.

Soda Is Sugar

With your physical ambitions, would you ever just eat 15 teaspoons of raw sugar? No? Well, that's exactly how much sugar is in a 12-ounce can of regular cola. Drinking two cans a day, or worse yet, a large fountain drink, could cause you to gain or maintain an extra 30 pounds per year!

BBQ Double-Veggie Burger Bowl

*If you do not have a grill but would like to host a BBQ style party,
multiply these ingredients and serve it as a BBQ casserole.*

1. Place frozen veggies in a bowl; microwave for 1 minute on high. Add Boca Meatless Ground Burger and microwave for another 2 minutes or until everything is hot.

2. Stir in barbecue sauce and enjoy!

Serves 1

100 calories
1g fat
10g carbohydrates
18g protein
459mg sodium
4g fiber

Ingredients
*1 packet Boca Meatless
    Ground Burger*
*2 tablespoons fat-free ricotta
    cheese*
*2 tablespoons marinara
    sauce*

Serves 1

130 calories
1g fat
20g carbohydrates
16g protein
440mg sodium
7g fiber

Ingredients
*½ cup frozen mixed
    vegetables*
*1 packet Boca Meatless
    Ground Burger*
1 tablespoon barbecue sauce

Toasted Cheese and Turkey Sandwich

Traditional grilled cheese sandwiches made with white bread, butter, and full-fat cheeses are loaded with saturated fats and gobs of unnecessary calories. This recipe is easier to make and far better for you!

1. Toast bread in toaster or toaster oven.

2. Place cheese and turkey between bread.

3. Microwave for 20 to 30 seconds.

4. Enjoy with a whole piece of fruit.

Serves 1

177 calories
0g fat
26g carbohydrates
23g protein
1,057mg sodium
6g fiber

Ingredients
2 slices light-wheat bread
3 slices fat-free American cheese
2 slices roasted deli turkey

Fitter PB&J

Make this old favorite healthy with wheat bread and fat-free fruit preserves instead of white bread and sugary jelly.

Spread peanut butter and preserves between bread and enjoy with a whole piece of fruit.

Serves 1

204 calories
9g fat
32g carbohydrates
8g protein
310mg sodium
6g fiber

Ingredients
2 slices light-wheat bread
2 tablespoons fat-free raspberry preserves
1 tablespoon peanut butter

Ham and Fruit

Lean meat and produce are the cornerstones of eating for a leaner body. If you're a busy person, combining healthy options in a simple way will lead to success.

Put ham on a plate and applesauce in a bowl. Enjoy with a peach!

Serves 1

223 calories
0g fat
38g carbohydrates
16g protein
1,159mg sodium
5g fiber

Ingredients
3 ounces fat-free deli-style ham, cubed
1 cup unsweetened applesauce
1 peach, medium

Rob's Grilled Chicken Sandwich

Serves 1

279 calories
3g fat
28g carbohydrates
40g protein
115mg sodium
9g fiber

Ingredients
2 slices light-wheat bread
1 Simply Grilled Chicken
   Breast (page 176), cooked
3 leaves romaine lettuce
2 tomato slices

This is a perfect go-to meal for the fitness enthusiast. If you forego fattening sauces like mayonnaise, you can find a grilled chicken sandwich almost anywhere!

1. Toast bread in toaster or toaster oven.

2. Layer chicken, lettuce, and tomato in between slices of bread.

3. Flavor with ketchup, mustard, or barbecue sauce.

Calorie Killers

If you're interested in finding some workouts that will torch a ton of calories in less than an hour, give running, rollerblading, kickboxing, jumping rope, and stair climbing a try. For a 160-pound person, these options burn more than 500 calories per hour; larger individuals will burn even more.

Teriyaki Chicken Power Pita

Teriyaki is the common Japanese term for grilled or broiled meat coated or glazed with a sweet soy sauce marinade.

1. Slice pita in half.

2. Chop chicken breast and mix with other ingredients in a bowl.

3. Evenly divide chicken mixture and place into separate pita pockets.

Restaurant Management

When you eat out, order healthy foods that resemble the ones you see in this book. Feel free to make special requests like holding the butter and oil, dressing on the side, and not bringing out the bread basket.

Serves 2

189 calories
2g fat
23g carbohydrates
21g protein
440mg sodium
3g fiber

Ingredients

1 large whole wheat pita
1 Simply Grilled Chicken Breast (page 176), cooked
½ cup chopped spring mix lettuce
4 tablespoons diced tomatoes
2 teaspoons white onions, diced
2 tablespoons sweet peppers
Dash of salt and pepper
2 tablespoons low-sodium teriyaki sauce

SWAT Sandwich

This sandwich is a favorite of one of the most athletic police officers and SWAT team members in the entire state of Florida.

Mix tuna and honey mustard together in a bowl. Spread mixture on each slice of toast. Top each slice with cheese. Bake in oven at 400°F for 1 to 3 minutes, or until cheese has melted.

Are You a Role Model?

If you are a parent or caretaker for young children, then you are a role model! Avoid degrading your body with words like "fat" or "ugly," and promote food choices based on creating a healthy body. To set a great example, you must treat yourself and your body with respect. Eat right, exercise, and speak in a positive tone.

Ultimate Veggie Wrap

Don't have alfalfa sprouts in your fridge?
Substitute broccoli instead. Use what you have.

Lay tortilla flat on a plate. Pile other ingredients on top of tortilla. Roll tortilla into a wrap.

"Conquer This" List
People rarely accomplish great things without a mission statement. You need to make one today, with a list of steps toward getting there. Get a dry erase board to write a list of fitness goals you plan to conquer. Make some small and some huge goals, and enjoy the process of checking off each triumph!

Serves 1

354 calories
10g fat
57g carbohydrates
11g protein
961mg sodium
4g fiber

Ingredients
1 12-inch spinach tortilla
½ cup spinach leaves
1 tablespoon tomatoes, diced
1 tablespoon mushrooms, sliced
1 tablespoon roasted red peppers
1 tablespoon green pepper slices
¼ cup alfalfa sprouts
1 tablespoon shredded carrots
1 tablespoon fat-free crumbled feta cheese
1 tablespoon balsamic vinegar

Chicken Burrito

Serves 1

317 calories
4g fat
43g carbohydrates
28g protein
526mg sodium
6g fiber

Ingredients

1 small whole wheat tortilla
½ Simply Grilled Chicken
    Breast (page 176), cooked
2 tablespoons black beans
1 teaspoon white onions,
    diced
2 teaspoons salsa
1 tablespoon shredded fat-
    free Cheddar cheese
¼ cup shredded romaine
    lettuce

Traditional burritos are loaded with rice. But with little nutritional value and lots of calories, rice is not the best idea for those in search of a flatter belly.

Place tortilla flat on a plate. Slice chicken breast. Pile remaining ingredients in the center of the tortilla. Roll tortilla up burrito style.

Goal Setting

Losing a dramatic amount of weight or completely upgrading your physique can seem like a daunting task. That's why it's vital to set short-, middle-, and long-range goals. For example, "Today I will avoid starchy carbs after 3:00 P.M." "I will lose two pounds by next week." "I will drop 7 percent body fat in six months."

Lentil Burritos

If you're a vegetarian looking for super sources of iron, lentils are one of your best bets. They're also a plentiful source of vitamin B₁, folate, and dietary fiber.

1. Wash and drain lentils. Bring lentils, broth, and water to a boil. Cover saucepan and simmer until lentils are tender yet holding their shape (25 to 40 minutes).

2. Sauté olive oil, onions, garlic, zucchini, and bell peppers over medium heat. When veggies are tender, stir in lentils, cumin, hot sauce, and taco sauce. Add salt to taste.

3. Stir in cheese until melted. Spoon ½ cup mixture into the center of each tortilla. Roll and serve.

Serves 6

492 calories
9g fat
78g carbohydrates
27g protein
1,216mg sodium
16g fiber

Ingredients

1 cup lentils, rinsed
2 cups low-sodium vegetable broth
1 cup water
1 teaspoon olive oil
½ cup white onions, diced
1 clove fresh garlic, minced
1 cup zucchini, chopped
1 cup red bell peppers, chopped
½ teaspoon cumin
¼ teaspoon hot pepper sauce
1 cup mild taco sauce
Salt to taste
4 ounces shredded reduced-fat Cheddar jack cheese
12 whole wheat tortillas

Naked Fajitas

Serves 1

321 calories
4g fat
8g carbohydrates
60g protein
322mg sodium
1g fiber

Ingredients
1 tablespoon yellow onions,
   sliced
1 tablespoon bell peppers,
   sliced
2 tablespoons frozen corn
1 Simply Grilled Chicken
   Breast (page 176), cooked
2 tablespoons shredded fat-
   free Cheddar cheese
1 tablespoon fat-free sour
   cream
1 tablespoon salsa

Fajitas can be fun. Although onions and peppers are the most traditional sort of veggies used to make them, you can grill up any sort of produce to go with yours.

1. Coat a skillet with nonstick spray. Cook onions, peppers, and corn on medium heat for 10 minutes. Slice chicken into thin strips.

2. Add precooked chicken to veggies and cook for 4 minutes. Place chicken and veggies on a plate and top with Cheddar. Serve with sour cream and salsa on the side.

Naked Mexican
The world pictures fajitas as a variety of meat and/or vegetables wrapped up into a flour tortilla, but you'd serve your abs well to go against the grain. Tortillas can add between 100 and 200 calories to your meal, so ditch 'em! Enjoy the flavors of Mexico without the evidence lingering around your midsection.

Fitz's Protein Power Potato

For added flavor, serve this potato with a one-ounce side cup of ketchup, fat-free sour cream, salsa, mustard, or barbecue sauce.

1. Bake potato in oven at 400°F for 15 to 20 minutes or in the microwave for 10 to 12 minutes or until the skin is crispy and inside is soft. Cut the potato in half. Cut chicken into small pieces.

2. Scoop out 90 percent of white potato pulp and discard it. Flatten out the remaining potato skin and put chicken in it. Sprinkle cheese on top.

3. Place potato back in the oven for 3 minutes. Remove potato from oven and top with lettuce and tomatoes.

Serves 1

259 calories
2g fat
36g carbohydrates
24g protein
149mg sodium
4g fiber

Ingredients

1 medium baking potato
½ Simply Grilled Chicken Breast (page 176), cooked
2 tablespoons reduced-fat shredded Cheddar mix
¼ cup shredded Romaine lettuce
¼ cup tomatoes, diced

Asian Lettuce Wraps

Serves 2

220 calories
5g fat
7g carbohydrates
36g protein
240mg sodium
2g fiber

Ingredients

*2 whole romaine lettuce
    leaves*
*2 Simply Grilled Chicken
    Breasts (page 176),
    cooked*
½ cup zucchini, shredded
½ cup carrots, shredded
½ cup cabbage, shredded
4 teaspoons peanuts
*1 tablespoon low-sodium
    teriyaki sauce*

*To add extra flavor to these wraps, pour 1 ounce low-sodium soy sauce or ginger
dressing into a small cup and dip wraps in it.*

1. Wash and separate lettuce leaves, place on a dish, and set aside. Slice chicken into strips. Mix zucchini, carrots, cabbage, and peanuts.

2. Evenly divide chicken strips and place in the center of the lettuce leaves. Evenly divide veggie mixture onto leaves, add teriyaki sauce, and wrap burrito style.

Double Dippers
Using lettuce in place of both breads and tortillas is a tremendous way to cut tons of calories. Each leaf of lettuce has about 1 calorie. One slice of bread or one tortilla can have more than 100 calories.

Chicken Philly

To save even more calories, exchange the sub roll in this recipe for a whole wheat pita. Serve with ketchup for the true Philly cheesesteak effect.

Serves 2

330 calories
4g fat
48g carbohydrates
31g protein
769mg sodium
4g fiber

1. Coat a skillet with nonstick spray and cook chicken strips on medium-high heat for 8 to 10 minutes.

2. Add peppers, onions, mushrooms, all-purpose seasoning, and garlic powder to skillet.

3. Cook for additional 5 to 8 minutes on medium heat or until chicken is thoroughly cooked and veggies are browning.

4. Divide and scoop chicken and veggies into each roll. Top hot mixture with a slice of cheese so it will melt inside the sandwich. Serve hot.

Cheesesteak Lore
The Philly cheesesteak sandwich is the pride of Philadelphia, Pennsylvania. It's traditionally based on steak and cheese with a hunk of bread, but that's not so good for your waistline; in fact, it's quite destructive. Always substitute for the fatty ingredients and make your own.

Ingredients

1 boneless, skinless chicken breast, cut into thin strips
¼ cup green bell peppers, seeded and sliced
¼ cup white onions, sliced
4 mushrooms
½ teaspoon all-purpose seasoning
½ teaspoon garlic powder
2 6-inch whole wheat sub rolls
2 slices fat-free American cheese

Healthy Veggie Cuban

This take on a classic sandwich uses lots of veggies and healthy toppings to provide a yummy lunch.

Serves 1

273 calories
4g fat
44g carbohydrates
16g protein
1228mg sodium
6g fiber

Ingredients

½ Portobello mushroom,
    sliced
¼ zucchini, sliced lengthwise
¼ yellow squash, sliced
    lengthwise
¼ red bell pepper, sliced
Salt and pepper to taste
1 4-inch portion Cuban bread
1 tablespoon Roasted Red
    Pepper Hummus (page
    156)
1 teaspoon yellow mustard
1 slice fat-free Swiss cheese
1 slice sour pickle

1. Coat a nonstick pan with cooking spray and add mushrooms, zucchini, squash, and red pepper on it. Season with salt and pepper to taste.

2. Bake veggies at 400°F for 8 minutes, flip veggies and cook for about 6 to 8 minutes or until brown.

3. Remove veggies from pan and refrigerate for at least 1 hour.

4. Slice Cuban bread in half. Spread hummus on top and mustard on the bottom.

5. Top bottom slice of bread with vegetables, cheese, and pickle.

6. Coat nonstick frying pan with cooking spray. Place sandwich in pan and cook each side for 3 minutes over medium heat.

Chapter 4
Snack Time

Bapoloneo Pops

Serves 6

149 calories
8g fat
17g carbohydrates
4g protein
79mg sodium
2g fiber

Ingredients
3 large bananas
6 popsicle sticks
6 tablespoons crunchy
peanut butter

These pops can be kept in the freezer for up to a week, and they're a great way to start your day. Breakfast on the go? You can't get more portable than this.

1. Peel and cut bananas in half lengthwise.

2. Press popsicle sticks gently onto flat side of each banana slice.

3. Freeze bananas on wax paper for 30 minutes.

4. Remove from freezer and spread one tablespoon of peanut butter on each banana.

5. Serve immediately or refreeze.

Snack Like a Smarty
To achieve and maintain a lean body, it's very important to make sure your snacks are just as healthy as your meals. Instead of grabbing snack bars, chips, or crackers on the go, always be prepared with healthy choices. Throw baby carrots, apples, and chicken breast cubes in a cooler pack and take them with you each day.

Peanut Butter Apple Slices

Peanut Butter Apple Slices are the perfect way to satisfy both your sweet tooth and your need for protein. This combination of protein and fiber will fill you up for quite a long time!

1. Core and slice apple six ways.

2. Spread peanut butter thinly over apple slices.

Serves 1

221 calories
9g fat
36g carbohydrates
4g protein
75mg sodium
5g fiber

Ingredients
1 large Gala apple
1 tablespoon peanut butter

Ants on a Log

Both peanut butter and raisins are very high in protein. The celery stalk is not only yummy, it's nearly calorie free. Use celery instead of crackers whenever possible.

1. Clean and chop the ends off of celery stalks.

2. Smear 1 teaspoon of peanut butter on each stalk.

3. Top peanut butter with 6 raisins per stalk.

Serves 2

262 calories
11g fat
39g carbohydrates
8g protein
244mg sodium
5g fiber

Ingredients
4 celery stalks
4 teaspoons peanut butter
¼ cup raisins

Tomato Time

This recipe is quick, inexpensive, and easy to whip up in 2 minutes at home. Make it before you leave in the morning and take it to work with you.

Serves 1

43 calories
1g fat
8g carbohydrates
2g protein
592mg sodium
2g fiber

Ingredients
1 large tomato
*5 sprays of Wish-Bone Salad
    Spritzers Caesar Delight
    dressing*
¼ teaspoon salt

1. Wash and slice tomato.

2. Spray tomato 5 times with Caesar Delight.

3. Salt to taste.

The Knockout!
The more you turn to produce for snacking, or even entire meals, the more likely you are to rid yourself of extra belly fat. Compare this tomato at less than 50 calories of pure nutrition to a snack bar filled with all sorts of hydrogenated oils for 150 to 200 calories, and you've got no contest!

Turkey Rolls

This simple snack is perfect for a day at the beach. It's light, healthy, and won't cause any tummy bloat while you sunbathe.

1. Place a piece of turkey flat on a plate.

2. Place half of a cheese slice in the center of turkey slice.

3. Roll up turkey and cheese.

4. Repeat for remaining ingredients.

Serves 1

93 calories
0g fat
8g carbohydrates
17g protein
913mg sodium
0g fiber

Ingredients
2 slices fat-free American cheese
4 deli slices roasted turkey breast, fat-free

Serves 1

241 calories
2g fat
58g carbohydrates
8g protein
466mg sodium
11g fiber

Ingredients
½ cup bran flakes cereal
½ banana, peeled and sliced
3 strawberries, stemmed and
    halved
½ cup skim milk

High Fiber Cereal and Fruit

Stick with a no-sugar-added variety of bran flakes cereal. The combination of high-fiber cereal, protein-packed milk, and nutritious fruit is a fun and filling choice for a quick snack.

Mix all ingredients in a bowl and enjoy!

Don't Overindulge on Healthier Snacks

One common weight-related pitfall is overindulging on foods labeled "low-fat." Low-fat foods are a good thing, but even foods labeled as such have calories. At the end of the day, weight management is based on calorie consumption. Enjoy low-fat foods, but stick with a single serving to reap the benefits.

Black Bean Treat

This snack tastes a bit like the bean dip you'd enjoy at a party as an appetizer. Not only is it delicious, it's easy to make and full of protein and iron.

1. Mix all ingredients except for Cheddar cheese in a microwave-safe bowl with a fork.

2. Cook in microwave for 2 to 3 minutes on high.

3. Remove bowl from microwave and sprinkle bean mixture with cheese.

4. Return to microwave for 30 seconds or until cheese is thoroughly melted.

Serves 1

176 calories
2g fat
23g carbohydrates
15g protein
748mg sodium
10g fiber

Ingredients
½ cup black beans, canned
2 tablespoons fat-free cream cheese
1 black olive, chopped
¼ teaspoon red wine vinegar
½ cup frozen spinach, thawed and drained
1 tablespoon salsa
1 tablespoon shredded fat-free Cheddar cheese

Pickles in Blankets

No, you don't have to be pregnant to enjoy this snack! Pickles in Blankets offer an indulgent combination of salty and creamy.

Wrap each pickle in a cheese slice and enjoy!

Serves 1

83 calories
0g fat
11g carbohydrates
11g protein
2,267mg sodium
2g fiber

Ingredients
2 large dill pickles
2 slices fat-free American cheese

Carrot Dippers

Bring this snack for a busy day away from home or the office. Fill a sandwich bag full of carrots and fill a small sealable container with your dip. Keep it in a cooler bag so when hunger strikes you'll be prepared.

Dip carrots in peanut butter and enjoy!

Keep It Simple

This recipe is ridiculously simple, but that's what keeps lean people lean. They know how to whip up something healthy in a hurry instead of resorting to fat-laden cracker packs or other traditional vending-style food. You can lose weight on a tight schedule; you just have to make smart choices.

Serves 1

134 calories
9g fat
11g carbohydrates
5g protein
110mg sodium
3g fiber

Ingredients

10 carrot sticks or baby carrots
1 tablespoon peanut butter

Chicken-Raisin Cubes

Chicken-Raisin Cubes are an ideal choice for snacks and lunches on the go. Place them in a plastic container and keep them cool. The protein will keep your energy high, and the raisins will satisfy your desire for dessert.

1. Cut chicken into large cubes.

2. Use a knife to dig small holes in the center of each chicken cube.

3. Fill hole with two or three raisins.

4. Serve hot or cold.

Serves 2

119 calories
1g fat
11g carbohydrates
17g protein
48mg sodium
1g fiber

Ingredients
*1 Simply Grilled Chicken
    Breast (page 176), cooked*
3 tablespoons raisins

Popcorn-Raisin-Nut Mix

Even low-fat microwave popcorn is traditionally high in sodium. The best way to enjoy popcorn as a truly healthy snack is to pop it with an air popper.

1. Pop popcorn with an air popper.

2. Combine popcorn with raisins and nuts.

Popping Up Pennies
Did you know you could buy twenty-five servings of popcorn for less than four dollars by buying popcorn kernels instead of microwaveable packs? Not only is using an air popper healthy, it ends up being the least expensive method as well.

Serves 3

147 calories
6g fat
20g carbohydrates
5g protein
3mg sodium
3g fiber

Ingredients
4 cups air-popped popcorn
4 tablespoons raisins
*4 tablespoons unsalted
    peanuts*

Cheddar Blasters

To change up this recipe a bit, you can substitute pears for the apple slices and Wasa crackers for the wheat. Change the cheese as well if you like, but stick with a fat-free variety.

Serves 2

243 calories
1g fat
21g carbohydrates
38g protein
903mg sodium
3g fiber

Ingredients
1 Red Delicious apple
2 slices fat-free Cheddar cheese
8 low-fat wheat crackers

1. Core and slice apple into 8 segments.

2. Cut each Cheddar slice into 4 pieces.

3. Place Cheddar on wheat crackers and top with 1 apple slice.

Dark Chocolate Pretzel Rods

To dress these rods up, drizzle colored melted chocolate lightly over the dark chocolate. You can find colored chocolate at a craft store, or even at Wal-Mart.

Serves 30

76 calories
3g fat
5g carbohydrates
1g protein
134mg sodium
0g fiber

Ingredients
30 large pretzel rods
8 ounces dark chocolate morsels

1. Melt chocolate morsels in a microwave-safe bowl for 40 seconds on high. Stir chocolate and heat for another 30 seconds. Stir chocolate and heat in 10-second increments until completely melted.

2. Holding one tip of pretzel rod, dip the bottom half in chocolate to coat.

3. Cool on a wire rack until chocolate is firm.

Sweet Spiced Pecans

These sweet snacks make a nice gift to give to friends, and they also work great as a protein-packed snack to eat on the go.

1. In a bowl, mix Splenda, cloves, cinnamon, and nutmeg.

2. In a separate bowl, coat pecans with egg white.

3. Toss pecans into spice mixture and coat thoroughly.

4. Coat a cookie sheet with nonstick spray.

5. Place pecans on cookie sheet and bake at 300°F for 30 minutes.

Serves 4

189 calories
18g fat
9g carbohydrates
3g protein
15mg sodium
3g fiber

Ingredients
¼ cup Splenda
1/8 teaspoon ground cloves
1 tablespoon cinnamon
1/8 teaspoon nutmeg
1 cup pecans
1 egg white, beaten

Sugar-Free Frozen Bars

Drinking calories is never a good thing for someone trying to become leaner. Crystal Light drinks are the perfect substitute for sugary juices, and they freeze up quite nicely as a snack.

1. Make your favorite Crystal Light drink as directed.

2. Pour beverage into frozen bar molds.

3. Add popsicle sticks and freeze for 1 hour.

Serves 8 ounces

5 calories
0g fat
0g carbohydrates
0g protein
0mg sodium
0g fiber

Ingredients
Crystal Light drink mix
Water
Popsicle sticks

Polka Dot Bars

Serves 8

51 calories
0g fat
12g carbohydrates
2g protein
18mg sodium
0g fiber

Ingredients

1 cup crushed pineapples in
    natural juices
8 popsicle sticks
1½ cups freshly squeezed
    orange juice
1 cup fat-free blueberry
    yogurt

To add polka dots to these bars, drop small pieces of fruit like maraschino cherries, cranberries, or grapes in each layer as you create them.

1. Pour pineapples evenly into 8 frozen bar cups. Freeze for 45 minutes.

2. Remove pops from freezer, insert sticks, and pour orange juice evenly into the cups on top of the pineapple juice. Freeze for 45 minutes.

3. Remove frozen bars from the freezer and pour yogurt evenly into the cups on top of the orange juice.

4. Freeze bars for 1 hour before serving.

Circuit Workout #1
Enjoy this quickie workout while your bars are freezing. Do 40 jumping jacks. Squat with your knees bent at a 90° angle and your back against a wall. Hold this wall squat for 60 seconds. Do 20 BOSU Rocks (page 13). Do 40 jumping jacks. Do 20 pushups. Do 10 V Sits (page 12). Repeat this series until your food is ready.

Berries and Cream

This dessert is both quick and simple. It's ideal for those in search of weight loss. One cup is filling, nutritious, and provides a bit of sinful satisfaction.

Place pudding in a bowl. Top with raspberries and stir.

Serves 1

56 calories
0g fat
13g carbohydrates
1g protein
332mg sodium
4g fiber

Ingredients
½ cup sugar-free vanilla
   pudding
½ cup raspberries

Fruit Jigglers

Sugar-free gelatin is the perfect sweet treat for someone trying to lose weight. Of course, fruit is best, but at 10 calories a serving, sugar-free gelatin will do no harm.

With a spoon, chop up gelatin in a bowl. Add strawberries to gelatin and blend together. Top with Fat-Free Cool Whip.

Serves 1

39 calories
0g fat
7g carbohydrates
2g protein
61mg sodium
2g fiber

Ingredients
½ cup sugar-free strawberry
   gelatin
½ cup diced strawberries
1 tablespoon Fat-Free Cool
   Whip

Candy Curse

When staring down the barrel of a junk food-loaded holiday, act strategically to avoid falling off of your weight loss wagon. For example, if you have to provide candy for Halloween or Easter, buy the kind you can't stand. Think sour candy is nasty? Buy it. You won't be tempted.

Chocolate-Covered Strawberries

Serves 12

94 calories
6g fat
12g carbohydrates
1g protein
2mg sodium
1g fiber

Ingredients

8 ounces dark chocolate morsels
12 large strawberries with stems

Eating an entire chocolate bar is definitely not smart when you're watching your waist. But enjoying a big, fat strawberry with a little coat of dark chocolate surrounding it is!

1. Melt chocolate morsels in a microwave-safe bowl for 40 seconds on high. Stir chocolate and heat for another 30 seconds. Stir chocolate and heat in 10-second increments until completely melted.

2. Hold a strawberry by its stem and dip the berry in chocolate to coat. Repeat with remaining strawberries.

3. Cool on a wire rack until chocolate is firm.

Chocolate-Covered Bananas

Serves 12

199 calories
6g fat
39g carbohydrates
2g protein
3mg sodium
4g fiber

Ingredients

8 ounces dark chocolate morsels
12 bananas, peeled and frozen

Freezing these bananas before you dip them is vital to give each banana the strength and stability to be dipped without breaking.

1. Melt chocolate morsels in a microwave-safe bowl for 40 seconds on high. Stir chocolate and heat for another 30 seconds. Stir chocolate and heat in 10-second increments until completely melted.

2. Hold each banana by one end and dip about 60 percent of the banana into the chocolate to coat.

3. Cool on a wire rack until chocolate is firm and refreeze until ready to serve.

Sweet and Nutty Granola

For a healthy snack at any time of day, keep Sweet and Nutty Granola stored in an airtight container for up to a week.

1. Preheat oven to 325°F. Coat cookie sheet with nonstick spray and set aside.

2. Mix the first four ingredients. In a small saucepan, mix water, honey, syrup, sugar, and oil. Bring to a boil. Add syrup to oat mixture and blend well.

3. Pour the mixture onto the cookie sheet and bake for 20 to 25 minutes, stirring every 5 minutes.

4. Pour granola mixture in a bowl and add cranberries and apricots. Blend together.

Serves 2

195 calories
5g fat
38g carbohydrates
4g protein
59mg sodium
2g fiber

Ingredients
½ cup regular oats
1 tablespoon almonds, slivered
¼ teaspoon cinnamon
Pinch of salt
2 tablespoons water
2 tablespoons honey
2 tablespoons sugar-free maple syrup
2 teaspoons Splenda brown sugar
1 teaspoon canola oil
¼ cup dried cranberries
¼ cup dried apricots

Chapter 5
Salads

Salmon-Spinach Salad

Serves 1

211 calories
7g fat
5g carbohydrates
30g protein
130mg sodium
2g fiber

Ingredients

5-ounce salmon filet, cooked
1 cup spinach leaves
½ cup red grapes
¼ cup shredded carrots
½ tablespoon sliced almonds
*1 tablespoon dried
    cranberries*

This salad makes perfect use of leftover salmon! Salmon will only remain good in the fridge for two days, so make sure you find a good use for it quickly!

Combine ingredients in a bowl and enjoy!

Buffalo Stomp Salad

Serves 1

185 calories
6g fat
7g carbohydrates
25g protein
119mg sodium
3g fiber

Ingredients

2 cups romaine lettuce
¼ cup plum tomatoes
¼ cup mushrooms
2 tablespoons sliced celery
1 tablespoon diced onions
*1 tablespoon shredded low-
    fat Cheddar cheese*
*3 ounces grilled chicken
    breast cut into strips*
*2 tablespoons Crystal Wing
    Sauce*

Unlike most wing sauces, Crystal is not made with butter. If you're going to purchase wing sauce, make sure you only buy the type with 0 grams of fat!

1. Combine all ingredients except for chicken and wing sauce in a bowl. In a separate bowl, coat chicken with wing sauce. Add flavored chicken to the salad.

2. Serve fat-free ranch dressing on the side if you choose.

Honey Bunny Salad

Honey-roasted turkey offers a unique sweetness, but you can substitute regular roasted turkey if you prefer.

Place all ingredients in a large bowl. Serve with a tablespoon of sweet dressing, such as fat-free raspberry vinaigrette, on the side if you'd like.

Tailgating for Tighter Tummies

Tailgating can be healthy if you choose it to be. Forget about packing regular burgers, chips, fatty dips, and beer in the cooler. Instead, bring chicken breasts or lean ground turkey burgers, fruits, veggies, baked chips, and salsa. Stick with one to two cans of light beer per person if you must, or just go for water and diet drinks.

Serves 1

379 calories
4g fat
73g carbohydrates
19g protein
993mg sodium
14g fiber

Ingredients

2 cups spinach
2 ounces honey-roasted
   turkey breast, sliced
4 tomato slices
1 tablespoon shredded low-
   fat mozzarella
4 red apple slices

Cordon Bleu Salad

Traditional chicken cordon bleu is horribly high in fat and calories. This dish will allow you to enjoy some of those flavors without paying too high of a caloric price.

Combine all ingredients in a bowl except for dressing. Serve with dressing on the side.

Diets Are for Dum-Dums
This book is a tool for healthy cooking designed to accompany a healthy lifestyle full of exercise. Diets are radical temporary solutions that only lead to temporary results. Don't do that to yourself! For true and long-lasting success, adopt healthy eating habits and make exercise a part of most of your days.

Serves 1

381 calories
5g fat
56g carbohydrates
35g protein
563mg sodium
9g fiber

Ingredients
2 cups romaine lettuce
2 ounces boneless, skinless
   chicken breast
1 ounce sliced deli ham
¼ cup plum tomatoes
¼ cup shitake mushrooms
1 tablespoon low-fat
   shredded Swiss cheese
1 tablespoon fat-free honey
   dijon dressing

Asian Chicken Salad

Use a prewashed, chopped, and ready-to-use bag of salad mix to save time.

Combine all ingredients except dressing in a bowl. Serve with dressing on the side.

Serves 1

187 calories
3g fat
16g carbohydrates
23g protein
204mg sodium
5g fiber

Ingredients
2 cups green leaf lettuce
3 ounces grilled boneless, skinless chicken breast
¼ cup plum tomatoes
1 cup alfalfa sprouts
¼ cup shredded carrots
1 teaspoon sesame seeds
2 tablespoons mandarin oranges
1 tablespoon sesame ginger dressing, fat-free

Tropical Cobb Salad

The mango, feta, and pine nuts in this salad offer incredible textural differences yet perfectly complementary flavors.

Combine all ingredients in a large bowl. Choose a low-fat citrus dressing to serve on the side.

Serves 1

181 calories
6g fat
9g carbohydrates
24g protein
174mg sodium
3g fiber

Ingredients
2 cups romaine lettuce
3 ounces Simply Grilled Chicken Breasts (page 176), cooked
¼ cup plum tomatoes
2 tablespoons chopped mangos
½ tablespoon toasted pine nuts
1 tablespoon feta cheese

Sweet Crusted Chicken Salad

Serves 1

349 calories
3g fat
50g carbohydrates
36g protein
319mg sodium
4g fiber

Ingredients
2 cups romaine lettuce
3 Sweet Crusted Chicken
   Nuggets (page 177),
   cooked
2 tablespoons raisins
1 tablespoon shredded low-
   fat Cheddar mix
¼ cup plum tomatoes
2 tablespoons shredded
   carrots

The Sweet Crusted Chicken Nuggets are best served right out of the refrigerator on this salad. If you chose to serve it warm, place the chicken on the lettuce and then sprinkle cheese on top.

Combine all ingredients in a bowl. Serve with a tablespoon of fat-free honey mustard dressing on the side if you'd like.

Slim Down with Sleep
Sleeping well is one of the best things you can do for your health. Well-rested people have more energy to exercise regularly. People with poor sleep habits are also less likely to eat healthfully. If you're serious about a healthy body, get a comfy bed and make sure you use it!

Greek Salad

The Greek diet is associated with a decreased risk of cancer. To pursue Mediterranean-style eating habits, enjoy olives, fruit, beans, and fish on a regular basis.

Combine all ingredients in a bowl. Serve with Greek dressing on the side.

Exercising While Injured

Unfortunately, life is full of mishaps and accidents. Sometimes injuries sideline us completely, and sometimes they only force us to be creative. Someone with a broken arm may be able to ride a stationary bicycle. A sprained ankle shouldn't keep a person from doing seated bicep curls either. Ask your doctor or physical therapist for some suggestions as you recover.

Serves 1

119 calories
6g fat
12g carbohydrates
6g protein
344mg sodium
4g fiber

Ingredients

2 cups romaine lettuce
¼ cup tomatoes, diced
2 tablespoons cucumbers, diced
2 kalamata olives
2 pepperoncini
2 tablespoons red onions, diced
¼ cup bell pepper slices
1 tablespoon feta cheese

Steak and Caesar Salad

Steak isn't always considered health food, but that doesn't mean you can never have it. Just make sure the steak you choose is lean, and pair it with truly healthful fruits and vegetables.

Serves 1

282 calories
10g fat
24g carbohydrates
14g protein
529mg sodium
2g fiber

Ingredients
2 cups romaine lettuce
2 ounces grilled, lean steak
½ tablespoon reduced-fat grated Parmesan cheese
2 tablespoons Fresh Gourmet Fat-Free Garlic Caesar Premium Croutons

1. Wash lettuce and chop to desired size.

2. Slice steak into strips.

3. Combine all ingredients in a bowl and serve with 1 tablespoon fat-free Caesar dressing *(optional)*.

Stay Sharp
If you store your knives in a knife block, always keep them cutting-side up. If the cutting side is down and against the wood, you'll dull them a little bit each time you remove them. This storage method will also save wear and tear on your knife block.

Taco Salad

Use caution when ordering this at a restaurant. Taco salads are often comprised of fatty ground beef, full-fat cheese, sour cream, and a fried tortilla shell.

Layer all ingredients in a bowl. Serve with salsa.

Salad Sabotages

For some reason, salads often tend to go terribly wrong. Here's how to avoid that wretched turn. Base your salad on veggies, fruits, and grilled meat. Never dump dressing on a salad; be a dipper instead. Take it easy on nuts, cheeses, eggs, pasta, and croutons. These things are high in fat, calories, or both.

Serves 1

233 calories
2g fat
34g carbohydrates
29g protein
462mg sodium
12g fiber

Ingredients
2 cups romaine lettuce, chopped
3 ounces lean ground turkey or Boca Meatless Ground Burger, cooked
2 tablespoons tomatoes, diced
2 tablespoons black beans
2 tablespoons onions, caramelized
2 tablespoons corn
1 tablespoon shredded low-fat Cheddar cheese
1 jalapeño pepper, sliced

Pepper Jack Caesar Salad

Traditional Caesar salads are based on romaine lettuce drenched in fattening Caesar dressing and topped with Parmesan cheese. Make these modest modifications and you'll enjoy all of the flavor with none of the fat.

Serves 1

283 calories
4g fat
28g carbohydrates
22g protein
728mg sodium
2g fiber

Ingredients

½ recipe Simply Grilled Chicken Breasts (page 176), cooked
1 tablespoon fat-free Caesar dressing
1 teaspoon green pepper sauce
2 cups romaine lettuce
2 tablespoons Fresh Gourmet Fat-Free Garlic Caesar Premium Croutons
1 tablespoon reduced fat shredded pepper jack cheese

1. Cut chicken into cubes. In a small bowl, blend Caesar dressing and green pepper sauce. In a large bowl, combine lettuce, chicken, croutons, and dressing.

2. Sprinkle with cheese and serve.

Preparing Cheese

To shred a soft or semisoft cheese, pop it in the freezer for about 30 minutes before grating to make it easier to handle. It also won't stick to the grater as much.

Ultimate Garden Salad

Garden salads often get a bad rap because they are usually made with iceberg lettuce. It's certainly not bad for you, but it's not very nutritious either. Stick with dark leaf lettuce and pile on the veggies for a fabulous garden salad.

Combine all ingredients in a bowl. Drizzle with balsamic vinegar.

The Evil Truth of Energy Bars
Did you know that some energy bars are truly no better than a regular candy bar? Some boast as much fat, sugar, and calories as a Snickers or Three Musketeers bar. Seek out bars that have less than 150 calories and are high in protein, low in sugar, and low in fat.

Serves 1

87 calories
1g fat
16g carbohydrates
6g protein
97mg sodium
6g fiber

Ingredients
*1 cup romaine lettuce
1 cup spinach, fresh
2 tablespoons diced bell
    peppers
2 tablespoons diced red
    onions
½ cup plum tomatoes
2 tablespoons diced
    cucumbers
1 tablespoon dried
    cranberries
½ cup broccoli florets
1 tablespoon peas
2 tablespoons carrots,
    shredded
1 tablespoon shredded low-
    fat Cheddar cheese
1 tablespoon balsamic
    vinegar*

Sweet Walnut Salad

Sweet Walnut Salad makes a splendid appetizer for many of the beef recipes in this book. To portion it as a starter salad, use this recipe to serve two people.

Combine all ingredients in a bowl and toss. Serve with fat-free raspberry vinaigrette on the side.

Tuna Salad

Served cold, this salad is the type of food that feels so good you can't believe it's actually healthy for you.

Place lettuce on a plate. Top with scoops of tuna and sliced tomatoes. Salt and pepper to taste.

Grilled Vegetable Salad

The crunchy vegetables in this salad complement the soft and sweet mango flavor brilliantly. Not only will you find it delicious, you'll enjoy its colorful appearance.

1. Treat a skillet with nonstick spray and place over medium heat. Add peppers, onions, and broccoli and sauté until brown. Sprinkle veggies with all-purpose seasoning as they cook.

2. Place veggies on lettuce in a bowl. Sprinkle with feta, nuts, and mango to top. Salt and pepper to taste.

Cool Fitness Tool: A Dog
Unlike that stair climber collecting dust in the corner of your bedroom, a dog is hard to ignore. Dogs need plenty of love, attention, and outdoor exercise! If you're willing to love one and care for it well, run to the pound and go running every day with the coolest fitness tool one could ever wish for.

Serves 1

75 calories
2g fat
12g carbohydrates
5g protein
97mg sodium
4g fiber

Ingredients
¼ cup red bell peppers, sliced (or green)
¼ cup yellow onions, sliced
1/3 cup broccoli florets
½ teaspoon all-purpose seasoning
2 cups romaine lettuce
1 teaspoon feta cheese
1 teaspoon pine nuts
2 tablespoons chopped mango
Salt and pepper to taste

Barbecue Salad

Serves 1

198 calories
3g fat
17g carbohydrates
26g protein
238mg sodium
5g fiber

Ingredients

1 cup shredded romaine
    lettuce
2 tablespoons tomatoes,
    diced
2 tablespoons cucumbers,
    diced
2 tablespoons bell peppers,
    diced
1 tablespoon shredded low-
    fat Cheddar cheese
3 ounces boneless, skinless
    chicken breast, cooked
1 tablespoon barbecue sauce
1 tablespoon garbanzo beans
1 tablespoon peas
1 tablespoon corn

When choosing lettuce in its original form or in a package, make sure to avoid leaves with brown edges and lettuce that looks excessively wet.

Combine all ingredients in a bowl and enjoy!

Go Barb

Barbecue-style restaurants traditionally serve very unhealthy food. Ribs, poultry with skin, fries, and biscuits are all belly-busting choices. If you find yourself at a BBQ joint, order grilled white meat without skin, butter-free veggies, and/or a salad. You can enjoy the flavor of a barbecue by using just a little bit of BBQ sauce on these healthier choices.

Sweet and Fruity Salad

Always rinse fresh produce under cool water. This will help remove things you don't want to eat such as pesticides, fertilizers, and bacteria.

Combine all ingredients in a bowl and enjoy!

Serves 1

135 calories
1g fat
33g carbohydrates
3g protein
18mg sodium
5g fiber

Ingredients
*2 cups shredded romaine
    lettuce
4 cherry tomatoes
½ cup Gala apple, sliced
2 tablespoons golden raisins
2 tablespoons mandarin
    oranges*

Broccoli Salad

This tantalizing salad makes a healthy, hearty side and helps spice up your entrée.

1. In a large bowl, combine first five ingredients and toss.

2. In a separate bowl, combine mayonnaise, vinegar, and Splenda.

3. Pour dressing over broccoli mixture and toss to mix.

4. Chill for at least 2 hours before serving.

Serves 6

130 calories
3g fat
27g carbohydrates
5g protein
551mg sodium
4g fiber

Ingredients
*5 cups fresh broccoli florets
1/3 cup raisins
¼ cup sunflower seeds
¼ cup red onion, chopped
1 cup frozen peas, thawed
1 cup fat-free mayonnaise
2 tablespoons vinegar
½ cup Splenda*

Chapter 6
Soups and Stews

Winter Vegetables Soup

Serves 6

191 calories
4g fat
34g carbohydrates
8g protein
1,141mg sodium
7g fiber

Ingredients

*2 cups frozen mixed
    vegetables*
2 cups zucchini, sliced
2 cups squash, sliced
1 cup yellow onions, diced
4 cups vegetable broth
2 cups diced tomatoes
1 teaspoon olive oil
*1 teaspoon fresh minced
    garlic*
*½ teaspoon all-purpose
    seasoning*
1 teaspoon fresh basil

Substitute chicken broth for the vegetable broth if you prefer. Go with a low-sodium version of either for the healthiest option.

1. Combine all ingredients in a large saucepan.

2. Cook on medium heat for 15 minutes.

3. Simmer for another 10 minutes, then serve.

Television Trauma
Beyond the fact that you're totally sedentary while watching it, television tends to be damaging to your health because of mindless snacking. In order to ward off the impact, avoid all buttery and salty options. Instead, choose low-calorie, high-fiber snacks such as carrots, berries, broccoli, celery, air-popped popcorn, and apple slices.

Black Bean and Corn Soup

To add flavor and spice to any of your dishes, add chili powder, jalapeño peppers, chipotle peppers, cayenne pepper, red pepper, or serrano peppers.

1. Combine all ingredients in a large saucepan.

2. Cook on medium heat for 15 minutes.

3. Simmer for another 10 minutes, then serve.

Black Beans

Black beans help lower cholesterol and are high in fiber, which helps slow rising blood sugar levels. Black beans are a particularly wise choice for people with diabetes or hypoglycemia. They are a virtually fat-free protein as well.

Serves 6

267 calories
3g fat
50g carbohydrates
15g protein
292mg sodium
15g fiber

Ingredients

4 cups black beans
1 teaspoon olive oil
1 clove fresh garlic, minced
½ teaspoon all-purpose seasoning
2 cups frozen corn
2 cups tomatoes, diced
2 cups crushed tomatoes
½ cup green onions, sliced
2 tablespoons chili powder
1 teaspoon cumin
½ cup bell peppers, diced
1 cup chicken broth
1 cup water

Extra Red Soup

Serves 4

189 calories
3g fat
39g carbohydrates
7g protein
826mg sodium
8g fiber

Ingredients

8 medium red bell peppers,
    seeded and sliced
1 cup yellow onions, sliced
1½ cups pumpkin, cubed
2 garlic cloves, crushed
1 green chili, chopped
1½ cups tomatoes, diced
2 cups vegetable broth
2 tablespoons fresh basil,
    chopped
Salt and pepper to taste

If you'd like to serve this soup cold, swirl 1 cup of plain yogurt into it just before serving for a creamy and delicious flavor.

1. Add bell peppers, onions, pumpkin, garlic, chili, tomatoes, and vegetable broth to a large saucepan and bring to a boil.

2. Simmer for 25 minutes or until bell peppers and pumpkin are soft. Drain, keeping vegetables and liquid in separate bowls.

3. Blend vegetables in a food processor and place back in saucepan with liquid. Add basil, salt, and pepper to soup and heat thoroughly.

A Better Body with Balance

To help your body thrive, remain lean, and fight disease, it's important to strive for balance. Seek out foods from various food groups each day, and aim for variety within each food group on a regular basis. Even though your favorite fruit may be apples, it's important to consume berries, citrus, and bananas as well.

Spicy Turkey Chili with Chocolate

The combination of smoky chipotle chilies and sweet
chocolate adds a deep, rich flavor to any chili.

1. Coat a large saucepan with nonstick spray. On medium-high heat, brown ground turkey with bell peppers, onions, garlic, and all-purpose seasoning, for 10 minutes.

2. Add remaining ingredients to saucepan and simmer for 15 minutes.

Chocolate in Soup?

Cocoa powder or unsweetened chocolate adds depth of flavor and richness to soups and sauces. Although most consumers associate chocolate with sweet confections, it isn't unusual to find it as an ingredient in savory dishes from Mexico, Central and South America. In fact, the national dish of Mexico, Turkey Mole, is built on a thick, chocolate-laced sauce. Chocolate or cocoa powder is especially good in vegetarian black bean dishes.

Serves 6

313 calories
7g fat
39g carbohydrates
25g protein
198mg sodium
9g fiber

Ingredients

2 cups lean ground turkey
½ cup bell peppers, diced
½ cup white onions, diced
1 clove fresh garlic, minced
½ teaspoon all-purpose
    seasoning
2 tablespoons Splenda brown
    sugar
1 teaspoon chipotle peppers,
    finely chopped
1 teaspoon cumin
3 cups pinto beans, cooked
1 cup tomatoes, diced
½ teaspoon black pepper
1 cup chicken broth
1 tablespoon cocoa powder
¼ cup sugar-free chocolate
    syrup

Veggies and Rice Soup

Serves 8

352 calories
5g fat
69g carbohydrates
9g protein
1,130mg sodium
7g fiber

Ingredients

2 cups instant brown rice
4 cups California-blend
    vegetables, chopped
1 cup Brussels sprouts, cut
    in half
2 cups sweet potatoes, peeled
    and cubed
4 cups vegetable broth
½ teaspoon all-purpose
    seasoning
1 clove fresh garlic, minced
1 teaspoon Italian herbs
½ cup yellow onions, diced
1 tablespoon olive oil
1 teaspoon oregano
¼ cup fresh parsley
½ teaspoon black pepper
1 cup celery, chopped
2 cups water

*To make this an even lighter soup with fewer calories,
reduce the amount of brown rice you use.*

1. Combine all ingredients in a large saucepan.

2. Cook on medium-high heat for 15 minutes.

3. Simmer for another 10 minutes.

4. Add additional water if soup dries out.

Boredom Leads to a Bulging Belly

Ever find yourself wandering mindlessly toward the refrigerator just because you have nothing else to do? You are not alone! Boredom can easily lead to belly fat if you're not careful. Keep a top ten list of things you'd love to do or have to do, and if you find some free time, get them done!

Chicken Soup Verde

It's very important to trim the bottom of the asparagus off or clean it very well. This portion of the vegetable often contains sand.

1. Wash and cut the woody end off asparagus, then cut into 1½-inch segments and set aside.

2. Add chicken broth and wine to a large saucepan and bring to a boil. Add chicken, asparagus, garlic, peas, and herbs to saucepan.

3. Simmer for 15 minutes and add sesame oil, noodles, soy sauce, and green onions to the saucepan. Simmer for an additional 10 minutes. Add salt and pepper to taste.

Spice It Up
Invest in a quality pepper grinder. The flavor of freshly cracked pepper is much cleaner and more intense than store-bought ground pepper. Read the directions on the pepper grinder, as many models are adjustable for the size of the grind.

Serves 4

272 calories
2g fat
18g carbohydrates
36g protein
772mg sodium
3g fiber

Ingredients
8 ounces fresh asparagus
4 cups low-sodium chicken broth
1 cup dry white wine
3 boneless, skinless chicken breasts, thinly sliced
½ teaspoon fresh garlic, minced
1 cup frozen green peas
¼ teaspoon parsley
¼ teaspoon dill
¼ teaspoon tarragon
½ teaspoon sesame oil
1/3 cup vermicelli rice noodles
1 tablespoon low-sodium soy sauce
½ cup green onions, sliced
Salt and pepper to taste

Tuscan Bean Soup

Tuscan cuisine combines a mixture of vegetables with the flavor of Mediterranean aromatic herbs.

1. Combine all ingredients in a large saucepan.

2. Cook on medium-high heat for 15 minutes.

3. Simmer for another 10 minutes, then serve.

Realistic Goals
Setting the bar high for your fitness is a great thing in most cases. Setting the bar too high initially may lead to feelings of failure and the desire to quit. Give yourself a break, set realistic goals, and achieve them at a realistic pace.

Serves 6

242 calories
4g fat
33g carbohydrates
14g protein
595mg sodium
9g fiber

Ingredients
1 clove fresh garlic, minced
2 cups zucchini, sliced
1 teaspoon oregano
½ cup bell peppers, diced
2 cups tomatoes, diced
1 teaspoon all-purpose
    seasoning
1 teaspoon cumin
½ cup carrots, sliced
1 cup red wine
3 cups white beans, cooked
4 cups chicken broth
½ teaspoon black pepper
1 tablespoon tomato paste
½ cup celery, sliced

Cannellini Minestrone

Cannellini beans are white Italian kidney beans, and they give this recipe a robust flavor. If cannellini beans are not available, they can be substituted with great northern beans or navy beans.

1. Combine all ingredients in a large saucepan.
2. Cook on medium-high heat for 15 minutes.
3. Simmer for another 10 minutes, then serve.

Ingredients

1 clove fresh garlic, minced
½ teaspoon all-purpose
   seasoning
3 cups cannellini beans
1 cup white mushrooms,
   sliced
½ cup white onions, chopped
½ cup celery, chopped
1 teaspoon dried parsley
1 teaspoon dried basil
½ teaspoon red pepper flakes
2 cups diced tomatoes
1 cup frozen spinach
2 cups water

Chickpea Soup

Chickpeas, also known as garbanzo beans, are loaded with folate, zinc, protein, and dietary fiber. It's a great idea for vegetarians to toss these little guys in meals throughout the week.

Serves 6

253 calories
4g fat
43g carbohydrates
14g protein
471mg sodium
6g fiber

Ingredients
1 clove fresh garlic, minced
1 cup bell peppers, diced
1 cup yellow onions, diced
3 teaspoons lemon juice
3 cups chicken broth
½ teaspoon red pepper
1 teaspoon ground ginger
½ teaspoon cumin
4 cups chickpeas, cooked
½ teaspoon all-purpose
*   seasoning*
2 cups carrots, sliced
3 tablespoons tomato paste
1 cup baking potatoes, cubed

1. Combine all ingredients in a large saucepan.

2. Cook on medium-high heat for 15 minutes.

3. Simmer for another 10 minutes, then serve.

Mindless Eating?
To keep yourself from eating too much at mealtime take the following steps. Make a habit of only eating while seated at a meal table. Avoid eating with distractions like the television. Chew your food slowly. Stop eating when you start to feel full.

Vegetable and Pasta Soup

To keep a quick and easy source of healthy veggies on hand, grab a huge bag of frozen mixed vegetables at a wholesale store and keep them in your freezer.

1. Combine all ingredients in a large saucepan.

2. Cook on medium-high heat for 15 minutes.

3. Simmer for another 10 minutes.

4. Add additional water if soup dries out.

Serves 6

259 calories
2g fat
52g carbohydrates
13g protein
465mg sodium
10g fiber

Ingredients

1 clove fresh garlic, minced
1 cup bell peppers, diced
1 cup white onions, diced
1 cup celery, sliced
3 cups chicken broth
4 cups frozen mixed
    vegetables
½ teaspoon all-purpose
    seasoning
¼ cup fresh parsley
1 cup baking potatoes, diced
2 cups whole wheat rotini
    pasta
2 cups water

Fall Minestrone Soup

Minestrone is the Italian name for a thick and hearty soup that often consists of legumes, veggies, rice, or pasta. The ingredients in this soup change with the season. Whichever vegetable is growing at the time gets used!

Serves 6

210 calories
1g fat
39g carbohydrates
13g protein
209mg sodium
9g fiber

Ingredients

½ cup yellow onions,
    chopped
1 clove fresh garlic, minced
½ teaspoon all-purpose
    seasoning
1 cup frozen peas
1 cup squash, sliced
1 cup green beans
1 cup carrots, sliced
2 cups white beans, cooked
1 cup chickpeas, cooked
1 cup frozen spinach
½ cup whole wheat pasta
1 teaspoon oregano
¼ teaspoon black pepper
1 chicken bouillon cube
3 cups water

1. Combine all ingredients in a large saucepan.

2. Cook on medium-high heat for 15 minutes.

3. Simmer for another 10 minutes, then serve.

The Indoor Walking Workout

If you enjoy walking for fitness, a rash of too cold, too hot, or too stormy weather shouldn't hold you back. The treadmill is an ideal exercise resource for when you can't go outside. You can also head to a shopping mall or even use your apartment building for an indoor adventure.

Carne Guisada

A lot of chefs choose beef tenderloin as their favorite cut of beef. It's quite lean and extremely versatile; cook it whole, slice into steaks, or cut small for stew!

1. Combine all ingredients in a large saucepan.

2. Cook on medium-high heat for 15 minutes.

3. Simmer for another 10 minutes.

4. Add additional water if stew dries out.

Buying Garlic

When buying fresh garlic, look for heads that are plump, firm, and heavy for their size. Any green shoots or sprouts indicate that the garlic is old and will have an off flavor. Store whole bulbs in an open plastic bag in the vegetable drawer of your refrigerator. Markets carry a variety of processed garlic options, but buy these in the smallest containers possible, since they lose their fresh taste and become stale very quickly.

Serves 6

248 calories
8g fat
13g carbohydrates
28g protein
541mg sodium
2g fiber

Ingredients

1½ pounds lean beef
    tenderloin, cubed
½ teaspoon all-purpose
    seasoning
1 clove fresh garlic, minced
1 cup tomatoes, diced
½ cup bell peppers, diced
1 cup tomato sauce
¼ teaspoon black pepper
½ cup cilantro, chopped
1 cup beef broth
1 cup baking potatoes, cubed
1 teaspoon oregano
1 cup sliced carrots
1 bay leaf
½ cup red wine

Tortilla Tomato Soup

Chipotle sauce is made from poblano chilies that are smoked. The smoking process tames the fire but intensifies the flavor of the chilies.

Serves 8

426 calories
8g fat
76g carbohydrates
17g protein
1,493mg sodium
8g fiber

Ingredients

½ cup red onions, diced
1 clove fresh garlic, minced
½ teaspoon all-purpose
    seasoning
4 cups tomatoes, diced
3 cups crushed tomatoes
¼ teaspoon black pepper
¼ cup fresh cilantro, chopped
3 cups chicken broth
3 cups whole wheat tortilla
    strips
½ cup shredded fat-free
    Cheddar cheese

1. Combine all ingredients except tortillas and cheese in a large saucepan. Cook on medium-high heat for 15 minutes. Simmer for another 10 minutes.

2. Toast tortilla strips in toaster oven until crispy.

3. Serve soup and sprinkle with cheese and tortilla strips.

Slow Down!

Did you know that it takes your stomach about 20 minutes to let your brain know it's full? For this reason, it's important for you to slow down and give your body a chance to do its job. Chew each bite slowly, savor the taste of your food, and stop when your brain says "enough!"

Three-Bean Chili with Veggies

Three-Bean Chili is the perfect chili recipe for those who want a hearty meal without beef or turkey. It offers a tremendous amount of protein and fiber but is low in fat and calories.

1. Combine all ingredients in a large saucepan.

2. Cook on medium-high heat for 15 minutes.

3. Simmer for another 20 minutes, then serve.

The Life of Spices
Make it a point to clean out your spice cabinet regularly. Dusty dried herbs and crusty, moisture-logged spices may not make you ill, but they won't do anything good for your cooking. Make it a point to toss any ground spices and herb blends that are more than three years old.

Serves 6

218 calories
1g fat
42g carbohydrates
13g protein
208mg sodium
13g fiber

Ingredients
1 clove fresh garlic, minced
½ teaspoon all-purpose seasoning
¼ cup carrots, diced
½ cup frozen corn
½ cup bell peppers, diced
½ cup zucchini, diced
1 teaspoon chili powder
½ teaspoon oregano
2 cups water
½ teaspoon cumin
1 cup tomatoes, diced
1½ cups pinto beans, cooked
1½ cups small red kidney beans, cooked
1½ cups black beans, cooked
½ cup tomato paste
1 teaspoon rice vinegar
2 tablespoons fresh cilantro, chopped

Moroccan Tagine of Chicken and Chickpeas

In Morocco, a traditional tagine is a stew cooked at very low temperatures so the meat has time to become very tender.

Add all ingredients to a large saucepan. Cook on medium high for 10 to 12 minutes, stirring often. Simmer for 8 to 10 minutes.

Label Reading
People often forget to check serving sizes when they read nutritional labels. For instance, a small bag of chips may read 120 calories per serving. Pay close attention and you'll know if that small bag is packing two servings and 240 calories.

Serves 6

264 calories
3g fat
22g carbohydrates
37g protein
260mg sodium
3g fiber

Ingredients

1 clove fresh garlic, minced
½ teaspoon all-purpose seasoning
2 teaspoons paprika
1 teaspoon ground ginger
½ teaspoon turmeric
1 cup yellow onions, chopped
2 cups tomatoes, diced
2 cups chickpeas, cooked
¼ cup cilantro, chopped
2 cups low-sodium chicken broth
6 boneless, skinless chicken breasts, cut in chunks

Creole Chicken Stew

Cayenne is an extremely flavorful, hot spice made from dried and ground peppers. It's used in a variety of cuisines and is quite famously used in hot sauces.

1. Combine all ingredients in a large saucepan.

2. Cook on medium-high heat for 15 minutes.

3. Cover and simmer for another 15 minutes, then serve.

Working with Onions
Refrigerate onions before cutting them to keep your eyes from watering. The cooling helps reduce the gases from emitting and irritating your eyes.

Serves 6

169 calories
2g fat
7g carbohydrates
29g protein
227mg sodium
2g fiber

Ingredients
*1 clove fresh garlic, minced
1½ cups bell peppers, diced
1 cup celery, chopped
1 cup tomatoes, diced
1 cup chicken broth
2 tablespoons parsley, chopped
1 teaspoon thyme
¼ teaspoon cayenne pepper
½ teaspoon all-purpose seasoning
6 boneless, skinless chicken breasts, cut in cubes
1 cup okra, sliced
½ cup yellow onions, chopped*

Asopao de Pollo

Sazon is a Spanish seasoning packet commonly used to flavor soups, stews, and beans. You can find it in the ethnic foods section of your grocery store.

Serves 6

242 calories
3g fat
30g carbohydrates
21g protein
133mg sodium
2g fiber

Ingredients
2 cups chicken chunks
1 clove fresh garlic, minced
½ teaspoon all-purpose
    seasoning
1½ cups tomatoes, diced
½ cup bell peppers, diced
½ cup yellow onions, diced
3 tablespoons green olives
½ cup cooking wine
1 Sazon packet
4 cups water
3 tablespoons cilantro,
    chopped
1 tablespoon oregano
1 cup brown rice, cooked

Add all ingredients except rice to a large saucepan. Cook on medium-high heat for 15 minutes, stirring often. Cover and simmer for 20 minutes. Add water if soup becomes dry. Add rice and stir to heat.

Fiscal and Physical Fitness
Credit debt and overeating are very similar issues. You should not spend more money than you have, and you should not consume more than you can burn off. Consider extra calories to be physical debt. Just like bills, you will have to work hard to get rid of them. Be conservative in both areas and you'll have health and wealth.

Red Lentil and Sweet Potato Soup

For a creamier soup, add 1 cup of fat-free sour cream or plain yogurt after cooking. Swirl cream and soup together gently.

1. Spray a large saucepan with nonstick cooking spray. Add onions and celery and cook on medium-high heat for 2 minutes, stirring often.

2. Add carrots, sweet potatoes, lentils, bay leaf, garlic, all-purpose seasoning, and broth to saucepan. Cover and cook on medium for 10 minutes.

3. Simmer for an additional 10 minutes. Remove bay leaf and blend soup in batches in a food processor.

4. Return soup to saucepan, add cilantro, and simmer for 5 minutes.

Serves 4

184 calories
2g fat
29g carbohydrates
12g protein
1,030mg sodium
7g fiber

Ingredients
*1 white onion, chopped
1 celery stick, finely chopped
1 large carrot, sliced
1½ cups sweet potato, cubed
1 cup red lentils, cooked
1 bay leaf
½ teaspoon fresh garlic, minced
½ teaspoon all-purpose seasoning
5 cups vegetable or chicken broth
2 tablespoons fresh cilantro, chopped*

Asian Soup with Tofu

302 calories
5g fat
54g carbohydrates
18g protein
554mg sodium
8g fiber

Ingredients
1 package firm tofu, cubed
1 cup shiitake mushrooms,
    soaked and sliced
½ cup canned bamboo
    shoots, drained and
    sliced
½ cup canned water
    chestnuts, drained and
    sliced
3 cups low-sodium chicken
    broth
1 tablespoon rice wine
1 tablespoon low-sodium soy
    sauce
1 teaspoon sesame oil
2 tablespoons rice vinegar
1 teaspoon ground ginger
½ cup green onions, sliced

Shiitake mushrooms are best when soaked in water for 25 to 30 minutes before cooking. Remove the hard stems.

1. Add all ingredients to a saucepan and bring to a boil.
2. Simmer for 15 minutes.

Tofu to You
Tofu is an ancient, protein-rich food from Japan, made by coagulating soy milk and pressing the curds into a cake. The process is similar to cheesemaking, and like cheese, tofu can be made in many forms and textures. Soft tofu can be whipped into drinks and desserts, while firm tofu can resemble meat in texture. Tofu has a very bland flavor, but easily absorbs the taste of other ingredients in a dish.

Veggie Burger Chili

For vegetarians and carnivores alike, ground veggie burger is an excellent food to keep in your freezer. It is low in calories and fat, offers a decent amount of protein, and can be cooked in 60 seconds!

1. Spray a large saucepan with nonstick cooking spray. Add oil, onion, pepper, celery, and garlic. Cook on medium-high heat for 6 to 8 minutes or until veggies have browned, stirring often.

2. Reduce heat to medium and add Boca Meatless Ground Burger to saucepan. Cook for an additional 5 to 7 minutes.

3. Add remaining ingredients to saucepan and bring to a boil, stirring often. Simmer for an additional 10 to 12 minutes or until thoroughly cooked.

Serves 6

215 calories
4g fat
29g carbohydrates
29g protein
1,129mg sodium
10g fiber

Ingredients

1 tablespoon vegetable oil
1 cup yellow onions, diced
1 cup bell peppers, diced
½ cup celery stalk, stemmed and diced
1 tablespoon roasted garlic
3 8-ounce packets Boca Meatless Ground Burger
1 (1.25 ounce) packet chili seasoning mix
4 cups canned chili beans, undrained
1 10-ounce can milder diced tomatoes and green chilies, undrained
1 cup tomato sauce
½ teaspoon all-purpose seasoning

Chapter 7
Appetizers and Hors d'Oeuvres

Chicken Wings

This dish is terrific served with Baked Tortilla Chips (page 117).
Unique for a dip, it stands alone as well.

Serves 10

262 calories
6g fat
9g carbohydrates
39g protein
948mg sodium
0g fiber

Ingredients
1½ pounds boneless, skinless chicken breasts, cut in cubes
1½ cups Crystal Wing Sauce
16 ounces fat-free cream cheese, softened
1 cup fat-free ranch dressing
24 ounces shredded low-fat Cheddar cheese

1. Coat a 9" × 13" baking dish with nonstick spray and set aside.

2. Boil cubed chicken breast until chicken is completely white through-out. Shred chicken with a fork and place it in the baking dish. Cover with wing sauce.

3. In a separate bowl, blend cream cheese and ranch dressing. Pour cream cheese mix over chicken. Sprinkle with Cheddar and bake at 350°F for 20 minutes.

Small Celebrations
Small physical achievements in fitness should be celebrated. If you've accomplished a goal like weight loss, strength gains, or completion of athletic events, rewarding yourself is a great idea. Just don't make food your reward. A new pair of shoes, a night out dancing, or a spa experience are fun ways to keep you celebrating in accordance with your goals.

Baked Tortilla Chips

Instead of stocking up with bags of oily chips and crackers, keep corn tortillas in the fridge and bake up an exact amount of chips whenever the need arises.

1. Preheat oven to 400°F. Cover two cookie sheets with nonstick spray. Cut each tortilla into 6 wedges. Scatter wedges onto cookie sheets.

2. Spray wedges with nonstick cooking spray and sprinkle with salt. Bake for 12 minutes.

Serves 10

52 calories
0g fat
11g carbohydrates
2g protein
156mg sodium
5g fiber

Ingredients
Nonstick cooking spray
10 fat-free corn tortillas
Salt to taste

Shrimp and Guacamole Tostada

To get creative with these tostadas, substitute grilled tofu, veggies, or chicken for shrimp.

1. Thread 4 shrimp on each skewer. Sprinkle each skewer with lemon juice, chili powder, salt, and garlic powder.

2. Grill shrimp skewers on a hot grill for 2 minutes on each side or until they turn bright pink.

3. Preheat oven to 350°F. Place tortillas on a cookie sheet and bake for 6 to 7 minutes.

4. Remove tortillas from oven and top each with 2 tablespoons Simple Guacamole, 4 shrimp, and green onions.

Serves 4

239 calories
10g fat
12g carbohydrates
25g protein
395mg sodium
2g fiber

Ingredients
16 jumbo shrimp, peeled and
    deveined (about 1 pound)
4 12-inch skewers
½ teaspoon freshly squeezed
    lemon juice
2 teaspoons chili powder
¼ teaspoon salt
¼ teaspoon garlic powder
4 small fat-free corn tortillas
1/3 cup Simple Guacamole
    (page 152)
1/8 cup green onions, chopped

Southern Skewers

Ingredients
4 12-inch skewers
*1 small yellow onion, cut into
    8 chunks*
8 cherry tomatoes
*½ green bell pepper, cut into
    8 chunks*
12 okra pods, trimmed
1 teaspoon olive oil
½ teaspoon sea salt
*½ teaspoon ground black
    pepper*
½ teaspoon water
¼ teaspoon chili pepper
1/8 teaspoon Splenda
1 clove fresh garlic, minced

Okra is naturally sweet and very high in fiber. Unfortunately, most people don't experiment with it. Try adding it to stews, stir-fries, and omelets.

1. On each skewer, thread 2 pieces of onion, 2 pieces of tomato, 2 pieces of pepper, and 3 okra pods.

2. In a separate bowl, mix the remaining ingredients well. Brush each skewer with the liquid mixture.

3. Place skewers on a hot grill and grill for 3 to 4 minutes on each side.

Computer Pal
Sometimes talking about weight- and body-related issues can be embarrassing to do with someone you know very well. Finding a friend through an online community like the one on WeightWatchers.com may help you find a confidant or two with whom you can discuss your progress freely and team up for encouragement.

Honey-Ginger Chicken Bites

Ideally, you'll allow this chicken to marinate overnight to intensify the flavors. For additional flavor, bring the leftover marinade to a boil in a saucepan then reduce to medium heat and simmer for 3 minutes to create a glaze.

1. Combine all ingredients in a container with a lid and mix well. Cover the chicken and let marinate for at least 1 hour.

2. Coat a cookie sheet with nonstick spray. Remove chicken from marinade and place on cookie sheet without crowding.

3. Bake at 425°F for 15 to 20 minutes, turning once.

Serves 4

161 calories
1g fat
25g carbohydrates
13g protein
409mg sodium
0g fiber

Ingredients

1/3 cup honey
2 teaspoons fresh ginger, minced
2 teaspoons lemon juice
2 teaspoons cider vinegar
2 teaspoons low-sodium soy sauce
½ teaspoon dark sesame oil
½ teaspoon freshly squeezed orange juice
1/3 teaspoon Worcestershire sauce
1 clove fresh garlic, minced
½ pound boneless, skinless chicken breast, cut in 1-inch cubes
½ teaspoon salt
1 teaspoon cornstarch
1 teaspoon water

Shrimp Cocktail

Serves 4

121 calories
2g fat
1g carbohydrates
23g protein
449mg sodium
0g fiber

Ingredients
2 quarts water
½ teaspoon salt
1 teaspoon lemon juice
*1 pound raw colossal shrimp,
    peeled and deveined*

Serve this shrimp with a squeeze of lemon juice for flavor or with Sweet Cocktail Sauce (page 153) in a cup on the side for dipping.

Combine water, salt, and lemon juice in a saucepan and bring to a boil. Add shrimp and cook uncovered for 3 minutes or until shrimp turn pink. Drain and rinse shrimp.

Hotel Gyms

Sometimes the fitness facilities in hotels are less than desirable. This is annoying, but it is an obstacle you can overcome. Suck it up and use the machines that are functional. If you don't like any, do equipment-free exercises like pushups, dips, crunches, lunges, and squats and then go for a run outside.

Roasted Veggies with Pine Nuts on Wasa

Pine nuts are a good source of both protein and fiber, and they add a rich flavor when added to meats, fish, and salads.

1. Coat a cookie sheet with nonstick spray. Place peppers, onions, and zucchini on the sheet and broil for 10 minutes or until blackened, turning once.

2. Remove vegetables from cookie sheet and cut into small pieces. Place in small bowl and set aside.

3. Coat a skillet with nonstick spray, mix remaining ingredients except for Wasa crackers and add to skillet. Cook on medium heat for 45 seconds.

4. Pour pine nut mixture over veggies and marinate for 2 hours at room temperature. Spoon veggie mixture onto each Wasa cracker. Serve immediately.

Serves 4

69 calories
1g fat
14g carbohydrates
3g protein
155mg sodium
3g fiber

Ingredients

½ cup red bell peppers, cut
    in strips
½ cup yellow onions, sliced
1 cup zucchini, sliced
1 tablespoon pine nuts,
    toasted
¼ teaspoon olive oil
Dash ground red pepper
¼ teaspoon fresh garlic,
    minced
2 teaspoons balsamic vinegar
1 teaspoon capers
Dash Splenda
Dash salt
4 Wasa crackers

Chicken Nachos

Bar food lovers rejoice! Skip the nacho dip while you're out and enjoy it when you're home. This recipe will satisfy that craving and then some!

1. Layer chips, chicken, and cheese in a large baking dish. Bake at 400°F for 5 minutes. Remove to a large serving dish. Sprinkle tomatoes over hot nachos.

2. Serve with peppers, sour cream, and salsa on the side.

Preparing Tomatoes

Core your tomato before cutting or dicing. Then season them with freshly ground black pepper and let them soak in the pepper for about 20 minutes. This gives the tomato the most pungent summer taste.

Serves 6

226 calories
3g fat
13g carbohydrates
35g protein
401mg sodium
2g fiber

Ingredients

4 cups Baked Tortilla Chips (page 117)
3 cups precooked grilled chicken breast, cut into small pieces
1 cup shredded low-fat Cheddar cheese
1½ cups tomatoes, diced
¼ cup jalapeño peppers, sliced
½ cup fat-free sour cream
1 cup salsa

Low-Fat Mexican O-Layered Dip

Always show up to a party with a healthy dish in hand. If the host has only provided unhealthy choices, you'll at least have one thing to enjoy!

1. Mix refried beans and taco seasoning, then spread onto the bottom of one large shallow serving dish.

2. Cover the beans with cream cheese, salsa, lettuce, Cheddar, onions, and tomatoes. Refrigerate at least 1 hour before serving.

3. Serve with Baked Tortilla Chips.

Try Something New
Branch out a little bit and expand your palate! In order to make produce a more prevalent part of your life, it's a great idea to sample something you've never tried before. Ever tasted an ugly fruit? It looks weird but tastes good!

Serves 8

129 calories
1g fat
18g carbohydrates
12g protein
684mg sodium
3g fiber

Ingredients
1 15-ounce can fat-free refried beans
½ packet taco seasoning
8 ounces fat-free cream cheese
½ cup salsa
2 cups romaine lettuce, shredded
1 cup shredded fat-free Cheddar cheese
¾ cup green onions, sliced
1 cup tomatoes, diced
4 cups Baked Tortilla Chips (page 117)

Stuffed Tomatoes

Serves 4

102 calories
1g fat
14g carbohydrates
10g protein
334mg sodium
2g fiber

Ingredients

*4 medium beefsteak
    tomatoes
¼ cup celery, finely chopped
¼ cup yellow onions, finely
    chopped
½ cup Gala apples, diced
    small
1 cup fat-free cream cheese
¼ cup fat-free sour cream
Salt and pepper to taste*

Instead of completely discarding the portion of each tomato you'll remove for this recipe, save it and use it later in a salad or stew.

Wash tomatoes thoroughly. Cut the tops off and scoop out the insides. Mix remaining ingredients in a small bowl. Evenly divide mixture and stuff tomatoes.

Tofu Treats

Serves 6

69 calories
4g fat
3g carbohydrates
6g protein
206mg sodium
0g fiber

Ingredients

*1 teaspoon sesame oil
1 pound extra-firm tofu,
    drained and cut into ½-
    inch cubes
1 tablespoon rice vinegar
2 tablespoons low-sodium
    soy sauce
¼ teaspoon ground ginger*

Tofu Treats have a really rich flavor and are best served on toothpicks. They're so good, you could actually even serve them for dessert.

Coat a skillet with nonstick spray. Add sesame oil and tofu to skillet and sauté on medium-high heat for 6 to 7 minutes or until brown. Remove tofu, mix with remaining ingredients, and chill.

Tuna-Stuffed Bell Peppers

White rice has nothing on wild rice. Wild rice has fewer calories and completely outdoes white rice with protein, B vitamins, potassium, niacin, and magnesium.

1. Wash bell peppers thoroughly, cut in half, and remove seeds and stalk. Place peppers on a cookie sheet and broil for 5 minutes on each side.

2. Mix rice, tuna, peas, Cheddar, basil, salt, and pepper. Stuff each bell pepper half with rice mixture.

3. Place pepper halves on cookie sheet; top with bread crumbs and Parmesan. Return to broiler and cook for additional 5 minutes or until golden brown.

Measure Your Middle
Although the scale is an effective tool for measuring progress with weight, it's not the only way to prove results. Take some measurements! Measure your waist, bust, chest, hips, thighs, and upper arms. These numbers will offer great proof of whether your belly is shrinking.

Serves 4

237 calories
2g fat
31g carbohydrates
24g protein
477mg sodium
5g fiber

Ingredients
4 medium bell peppers
1½ cups wild rice, cooked
7 ounces white tuna in water
½ cup canned green peas, drained
½ cup shredded fat-free Cheddar cheese
½ teaspoon basil
Salt and pepper to taste
2 tablespoons dry bread crumbs
1 tablespoon Parmesan cheese

Sweet Potato and Cassava Chips

To add a variety of flavors to your chips, substitute paprika, curry powder, chili powder, or Parmesan cheese in place of the garlic powder and sea salt.

Serves 4

410 calories
2g fat
94g carbohydrates
4g protein
155mg sodium
6g fiber

Ingredients

*2 large sweet potatoes,
    peeled
2 large cassavas, peeled
½ tablespoon olive oil
¼ teaspoon garlic powder
¼ teaspoon sea salt*

1. Thinly slice sweet potatoes and cassavas so they resemble potato chips. Gently combine potato and cassava slices with oil, garlic powder, and sea salt.

2. Coat a cookie sheet with nonstick spray. Place chips on cookie sheet and bake at 400°F for 10 to 20 minutes or until lightly brown and crisp.

Pita Chips

Change the flavor of your pita chips by adding a variety of toppings such as garlic and herbs, chili pepper, cinnamon, or Parmesan cheese.

Serves 4

86 calories
1g fat
18g carbohydrates
3g protein
170mg sodium
2g fiber

Ingredients

*2 whole wheat pitas
¼ teaspoon garlic powder*

Cut each pita into 8 wedges. Place wedges on cookie sheet and sprinkle with garlic powder. Bake at 350°F for 10 to 15 minutes or until lightly brown and crisp.

Potato Skins

Tough-skinned items like potatoes should be scrubbed with a vegetable brush under cool running water. Once clean, pat them dry with paper towels.

1. Cut potatoes in half and scoop out 90 percent of the pulp. Coat a large cookie sheet with nonstick spray.

2. Place potato halves on sheet and sprinkle with salt and pepper. Bake potatoes at 475°F for 10 to 15 minutes or until crispy.

3. Sprinkle potatoes with cheese and return to oven for 2 minutes. Sprinkle potatoes with onions and serve with a dollop of sour cream.

Keep a Food Diary
Studies show most people dramatically underestimate their caloric consumption each day. To investigate the truth, keep a detailed food diary for one whole week. Write down every single bite you eat, what sauce you use, and what beverages you drink. If you suck on a mint, write it down.

Serves 6

173 calories
0g fat
36g carbohydrates
8g protein
271mg sodium
3g fiber

Ingredients
6 medium baking potatoes, washed
½ teaspoon salt
1/8 teaspoon black pepper
½ cup fat-free shredded Cheddar cheese
¼ cup green onions, sliced
½ cup fat-free sour cream

Tomatoes on Wasa

Wasa crackers are a Swedish invention.
They are baked crisp crackers made from whole grains.
Their long shape is perfect for holding a variety of dips and toppings.

Serves 4

60 calories
1g fat
12g carbohydrates
12g protein
91mg sodium
3g fiber

Ingredients

1 cup Roma tomatoes,
*   chopped*
1 tablespoon fresh basil,
*   chopped*
1 teaspoon capers
½ teaspoon balsamic vinegar
½ tablespoon olive oil
¼ teaspoon fresh garlic,
*   minced*
Sea salt and pepper to taste
4 Wasa crackers

Mix all ingredients except for crackers. Top each Wasa cracker with tomato mixture.

Baby Steps
Quitting unhealthy habits cold turkey may be a great idea, but this method rarely works. To ditch that belly fat, start by setting small, attainable goals. Plan to avoid alcoholic beverages tonight, or exercise for 30 minutes this afternoon. Slowly add great habits to your life and lose bad ones.

Grilled Vegetable Salad

This veggie salad can be grilled and chilled the night before serving to intensify flavors.

1. Heat a grill or electric griddle. Place all vegetables on grill and cook for 10 to 12 minutes, turning occasionally.

2. Remove veggies from the grill, cut them into smaller pieces, and place in a bowl. In a separate bowl add remaining ingredients and whisk well.

3. Pour mixture over veggies and cover. Refrigerate at least 2 hours before serving.

Nag, Nag, Nag

Do you love someone who doesn't share the same ambition for health as you do? Unfortunately, nagging won't get them to comply. Nobody likes to be bullied. Instead, be supportive, show compassion, and be an inspiring role model.

Serves 4

56 calories
2g fat
11g carbohydrates
2g protein
140mg sodium
4g fiber

Ingredients
2 medium red bell peppers, cut in wide strips
2 medium zucchini, sliced lengthwise
1 medium eggplant (½-pound), cut in half lengthwise
2 medium yellow squash, sliced lengthwise
¼ cup fresh parsley, chopped
¼ cup balsamic vinegar
1 teaspoon extra-virgin olive oil
¼ teaspoon salt
1 clove fresh garlic, minced

Chipotle and Citrus Lime Salad

Green onions, also known as scallions, are onions that have tiny bulbs and long green stalks. Eat them raw, grilled, or sautéed.

Serves 4

69 calories
1g fat
8g carbohydrates
7g protein
208mg sodium
1g fiber

Ingredients

*2 tablespoons fat-free
    mayonnaise*
*¼ teaspoon chopped chipotle
    chili in Adobo sauce*
1 teaspoon lime juice
¼ pound crab meat
*1 tablespoon grated low-fat
    Parmesan cheese*
*1 tablespoon water
    chestnuts, finely chopped*
*1 tablespoon green onions,
    finely chopped*
*1 tablespoon fresh cilantro,
    finely chopped*
*1 tablespoon red bell
    peppers, finely chopped*
12 baked tortilla or pita chips

1. Whisk together mayonnaise, chili, and lime juice. In a separate bowl, mix remaining ingredients except the chips with a fork.

2. Add mayonnaise mixture to crab mixture and blend well. Lay chips on a cookie sheet and spoon 1 tablespoon crab mixture on top of each chip.

3. Bake at 350°F for 5 minutes and serve warm.

Salmon Quesadilla

Salmon is easily found in most grocery stores in vacuum-packed pouches and cans. Salmon is a great source of calcium and omega-3 and omega-6 fatty acids.

1. Mix all ingredients except tortillas. Spread salmon mixture over half of each tortilla.

2. Fold tortilla over and cook in nonstick skillet over medium heat for 2 minutes on each side. Cut each quesadilla into three wedges and serve.

Kicking Calories
Kickboxing is a fantastic activity for burning tons of calories and tightening up your core. The effort it takes to punch and kick a heavy bag repeatedly requires a massive amount of energy. The process of rotating to throw proper strikes forces your abdominals and lower back to contract and flex consistently as well.

Serves 4

262 calories
6g fat
28g carbohydrates
22g protein
1,149mg sodium
2g fiber

Ingredients
1/3 cup fat-free cream cheese
¼ cup white onions, finely chopped
¼ teaspoon fresh garlic, minced
12 ounces smoked salmon, chopped
1/8 teaspoon ground pepper
4 8-inch whole wheat tortillas

Pineapple and Grape Skewers

Serves 4

109 calories
1g fat
28g carbohydrates
1g protein
9mg sodium
3g fiber

Ingredients

1 fresh pineapple, cored,
    peeled
16 large seedless grapes
8 wooden 12-inch skewers
2 tablespoons lemon juice

When you grill with wooden skewers, soak skewers in water at least 30 minutes before cooking to prevent the wood from burning.

1. Cut pineapple into 1-inch cubes. Thread pineapple cubes and grapes onto 8 medium sized skewers, alternating the fruit. Drizzle with lemon juice.

2. Heat grill to medium heat and cook skewers 6 to 8 minutes or until lightly brown, turning occasionally. Serve with Light Lemony Yogurt Sauce (page 153).

Chapter 8
Side Dishes

Citrus-Glazed Green Beans

Serves 4

66 calories
0g fat
18g carbohydrates
3g protein
158mg sodium
5g fiber

Ingredients

*1 large Vidalia onion, thinly
    sliced*
2 teaspoons Splenda
*1 pound green beans,
    trimmed*
*¼ cup sugar-free orange
    marmalade*
½ teaspoon ground ginger
*1 tablespoon low-sodium soy
    sauce*

If you are short on time, cover the onions while you cook them to achieve the same caramelizing effect. Keep an eye on the onions and remove once they brown. This may take 8 to 12 minutes.

1. Coat a skillet with nonstick spray. Add oil, onions, and Splenda to skillet and cook on medium heat for 25 minutes or until onions are browned.

2. Meanwhile, cook green beans in boiling water for 4 to 5 minutes. Remove tender beans to a bowl of ice cold water and drain.

3. Add green beans to skillet with onions. Add marmalade, ginger, and soy sauce to skillet and stir well. Cook for 4 to 7 minutes until sauce has thickened and food is hot.

Fruit and Cabbage Slaw

Cabbage is incredibly high in fiber, and this slaw makes a sweet and light side dish for almost any meal.

1. In a large bowl, combine cabbage, apple, pear, onions, and pecans. In a separate bowl, whisk together honey, cider, and vinegar.

2. Pour honey dressing over slaw and toss. Sprinkle with parsley. Chill and serve.

Serves 4

117 calories
3g fat
24g carbohydrates
2g protein
23mg sodium
5g fiber

Ingredients

1 pound cabbage, shredded
1 Granny Smith apple, chopped
1 pear, chopped
¼ cup chopped red onions
2 tablespoons candied pecans
1½ teaspoons honey
¼ cup apple cider
¼ cup cider vinegar
1 tablespoon parsley, finely chopped

Spaghetti Squash

Spaghetti squash truly takes on the qualities of pasta noodles. Flavor it with marinara, low-sodium soy and teriyaki sauces, or anything else you traditionally add to regular pasta.

1. Slice squash in half and scoop out the seeds. Wrap each half in plastic wrap. Cook wrapped squash in microwave for 20 minutes on high power. Remove plastic wrap.

2. Using a fork, scoop squash into a medium bowl. The squash should be stringy like spaghetti.

Serves 4

70 calories
1g fat
16g carbohydrates
1g protein
39mg sodium
0g fiber

Ingredients

1 2-pound spaghetti squash

Low-Fat Cheese Fries

Choose the lowest-fat version of French fries you can find. Jazz this recipe up a bit with a little cayenne pepper, chili powder, or a variety of different fat-free cheeses.

Serves 4

176 calories
4g fat
27g carbohydrates
8g protein
130mg sodium
2g fiber

Ingredients

12 ounces crinkle cut frozen French fried potatoes
½ cup fat-free shredded Cheddar cheese
Salt
4 tablespoons ketchup
4 tablespoons fat-free sour cream

1. Bake fries on a nonstick baking sheet at 450°F for 15 to 20 minutes, flipping fries once. Remove fries from oven and sprinkle with cheese.

2. Bake for 3 more minutes or until cheese has melted. Dress with salt, ketchup, or sour cream as desired.

Forbidden Fries

A 130-pound woman would have to run 3 miles at 6 miles per hour in order to burn off the calories in a medium order of McDonald's french fries. Wouldn't it be easier to skip the French fries all together? You can easily consume lots of calories; burning lots of calories off is hard work!

Asparagus Salad

When selecting your asparagus, look for straight, firm stalks with tightly closed tips. You'll need to peel the asparagus if the stalks are too thick and woody.

1. Coat a skillet with nonstick spray. Add asparagus, and all-purpose seasoning to skillet.

2. Toss gently and cook asparagus on medium-high heat for 5 minutes. Remove asparagus to a large serving dish.

3. Top with remaining vegetables and drizzle with vinaigrette.

Step It Up

A pedometer is one of the simplest tools you can use to enhance your overall fitness level. A popular program asks people to walk or run at least 10,000 steps per day. This is a smart, precise way to monitor your fitness. Once you hit 10,000 steps, amp your average up to 11,000 or more!

Serves 4

46 calories
0g fat
10g carbohydrates
3g protein
162mg sodium
3g fiber

Ingredients
2 pounds asparagus, woody ends cut off
½ teaspoon all-purpose seasoning
10 cherry tomatoes, quartered
1 cup cucumber, diced
½ cup green onions, sliced
¼ cup fat-free vinaigrette

Crunchy and Colorful Veggies

*Since corn kernels are so small, the frozen variety heats up
quite quickly without requiring much time to thaw. This often makes
it a simple and convenient choice.*

Serves 6

75 calories
0g fat
16g carbohydrates
3g protein
26mg sodium
4g fiber

Ingredients

*2 cups bell peppers, seeded
and sliced*
2 cups sugar snap peas
1 cup frozen corn
2 cups white onions, chopped
*½ teaspoon all-purpose
seasoning*

1. Coat a skillet with nonstick spray. Place all veggies in skillet and sprinkle with all-purpose seasoning.

2. Cook on medium high for 15 to 20 minutes or until veggies are tender, stirring often.

Colorful Squash and Green Beans

*Did you know that green beans are helpful in maintaining bone density?
They're a super source of vitamins C and K.*

Serves 6

34 calories
0g fat
8g carbohydrates
2g protein
25mg sodium
3g fiber

Ingredients

*6 cups multicolored squash,
sliced*
2 cups green beans
*½ teaspoon all-purpose
seasoning*
Salt and pepper to taste

Heat a large skillet on the stove at medium heat. Toss ingredients in skillet and cook until veggies are tender and browning. Salt and pepper to taste.

Sweet Stuffed Sweet Potatoes

Store sweet potatoes in a cool dry place; they do not need to be refrigerated.

1. Pierce sweet potatoes with sharp knife and bake 25 minutes at 400°F. Cut potatoes in half lengthwise. Scoop out 80 percent of potato pulp.

2. In a large bowl, combine potato pulp with remaining ingredients. Stir mixture with a fork until well blended. Divide mixture and place back into potato skins.

3. Bake potatoes in a pan at 350°F for 15 minutes.

Simpler Side of Sweet Potatoes
Sweet potatoes are packed with potassium, vitamin A, and vitamin C. Cut a few holes in one, zap it in the microwave, and enjoy for lunch. No need to be fancy; this potato is divine all on its own.

Serves 4

85 calories
0g fat
20g carbohydrates
1g protein
9mg sodium
2g fiber

Ingredients
2 large sweet potatoes
½ cup canned syrup-free crushed pineapples, drained
¼ teaspoon vanilla extract
¼ teaspoon ground cinnamon
1 teaspoon firmly packed Splenda brown sugar

Colorful Vegetable Teriyaki

Serves 4

228 calories
1g fat
55g carbohydrates
9g protein
379mg sodium
10g fiber

Ingredients

1 cup broccoli florets
1 cup sugar snap peas
½ cup sliced water chestnuts,
   drained
½ cup baby corn, drained
1 cup cauliflower, in chunks
1 cup shiitake mushrooms,
   sliced
1/3 cup low-sodium teriyaki
   sauce

If you prefer to use frozen vegetables instead of fresh, you may have to increase your cooking time to allow for thawing.

1. Coat a skillet with nonstick spray. Add all ingredients, except teriyaki sauce, to skillet.

2. Cook vegetables for 15 minutes on medium high or until broccoli is tender. Pour teriyaki on veggies and simmer for 3 minutes.

More about Mushrooms

Did you know that shiitake mushrooms traditionally sprout off of logs? They're the most common type of mushroom used in Asian dishes, and they add a deep flavor and chewy texture. If you prefer an even more intense flavor from your mushrooms, buy your shiitake mushrooms dried instead of fresh.

French "Fried" Carrot Sticks

You could purchase already peeled and cut carrot sticks at your market. If you choose to go with large carrots, make sure you wash, peel, and cut them into sticks before cooking.

1. Combine all ingredients in a large bowl and coat carrots evenly. Cover a large cookie sheet with nonstick spray. Place carrots on sheet, being careful not to crowd them.
2. Bake at 425°F for 18 to 22 minutes or until carrots are tender and brown.

Serves 6

137 calories
3g fat
28g carbohydrates
3g protein
450mg sodium
8g fiber

Ingredients

4 pounds carrot sticks
1 tablespoon olive oil
2 tablespoons chopped fresh rosemary
2 teaspoons Splenda
1 teaspoon salt
¼ teaspoon pepper

Roasted Zucchini and Squash

Both yellow squash and zucchini are summer squashes. Unlike winter squashes, these can be eaten raw.

1. Slice vegetables lengthwise into thin strips. Coat a cookie sheet with nonstick spray. Lay veggie strips on cookie sheet, being careful not to crowd them.
2. Sprinkle with all-purpose seasoning. Bake in 375°F oven for 16 minutes, flipping once.

Serves 6

33 calories
0g fat
7g carbohydrates
2g protein
25mg sodium
3g fiber

Ingredients

3 zucchini
3 yellow squash
½ teaspoon all-purpose seasoning

Caramelized Onions

Studies show that onions can significantly cut the risk of blood clots. They contain sulfides, which are known to lower blood pressure and blood lipids.

Serves 6

21 calories
0g fat
5g carbohydrates
1g protein
22mg sodium
1g fiber

Ingredients

3 yellow onions, peeled and
    sliced
½ teaspoon all-purpose
    seasoning

1. Coat a skillet with nonstick spray. Add onion slices and all-purpose seasoning to the skillet. Cook on medium-high heat for 10 minutes, stirring often.

2. Onions are done when they are tender and brown.

Cut One Thing Out

What's the one thing in your day that could possibly be responsible for your body retaining just a little bit of weight? Is it the syrup in your morning coffee? Could it be the mini muffin you allow yourself after lunch? How about that ritualistic nighttime snack? Cut this item out and see how your body responds.

Baked Sweet Potato Fries

Baked Sweet Potato Fries are a nutritional step up from regular baked fries for sure. Having said that, they're not too fancy for ketchup!

1. Preheat oven to 450°F. Cut potatoes into matchsticks, about ½-inch thick. Toss potatoes, cinnamon, and olive oil in a bowl.

2. Coat a large cookie sheet with nonstick spray. Bake for 25 to 30 minutes or until potatoes are fairly crispy.

Dressing Out

A common thread amongst fitness success stories is that they all dress out for fitness no matter what. Even after a hard day's work, these people put on their workout gear to help get them in the mood. Throw on some shorts and sneakers and see if it works for you too!

Serves 6

136 calories
3g fat
27g carbohydrates
2g protein
14mg sodium
4g fiber

Ingredients
2 pounds peeled sweet potatoes
2 teaspoons ground cinnamon
1 tablespoon olive oil

Sweet and Sour Baby Carrots

This recipe is served as a cold side dish, so spend time making it the night before you plan to serve it. As a last resort, make it the morning before your dinner.

Serves 6

91 calories
1g fat
28g carbohydrates
2g protein
581mg sodium
4g fiber

Ingredients

2 pounds baby carrots
4 cups boiling water
1 cup Splenda
½ cup cider vinegar
1 teaspoon salt
1 tablespoon yellow mustard
1 tablespoon Worcestershire
*   sauce*
1 white onion, chopped
1 green bell pepper, chopped
1 cup canned tomato soup

1. In a large saucepan, boil carrots in water until carrots are tender. Drain carrots.

2. In a medium saucepan, combine Splenda, vinegar, salt, mustard, and Worcestershire sauce on medium-high heat.

3. Bring Splenda mixture to a boil and add onion, pepper, and soup. Add tender carrots to the mixture and return to a boil. Remove from heat and cool.

4. Seal carrot dish in a container and refrigerate at least 3 hours before serving.

Crispy Squash Casserole

If you love this recipe but are looking for a change, try substituting zucchini for the yellow squash. These vegetables are traditionally interchangeable because of similar flavors and textures.

Serves 6

122 calories
3g fat
14g carbohydrates
11g protein
601mg sodium
5g fiber

Ingredients
10 medium yellow squash, sliced
1 yellow onion, chopped
1 teaspoon salt
Pinch black pepper
6 ounces shredded fat-free Cheddar cheese
½ cup Egg Beaters
10 low-fat, whole wheat crackers, crushed

1. Coat a 9" × 13" baking dish with nonstick spray. Place squash and onion in dish. Sprinkle with salt and pepper and bake at 350°F for 15 minutes.

2. Drain water from veggies and stir in cheese. Cool for 10 minutes. Mix Egg Beaters into veggies. Stir in crackers until thick.

3. Return dish to oven and bake at 325°F for 30 minutes.

Playing at the Park
Although structured workouts are fantastic, it's often nice to just go play. Did you know that you could easily burn several hundred calories just by running around a playground with some active children? Playing chase, pushing the merry-go-round, and climbing stairs may serve as a perfect yet productive change of routine.

Zucchini Casserole

This casserole not only serves as a delicious side dish, it is filling enough to serve as an entire vegetarian entrée. As an entrée it should provide 3 servings.

Serves 6

111 calories
2g fat
17g carbohydrates
7g protein
486mg sodium
3g fiber

Ingredients

1 clove fresh garlic, minced
1 teaspoon olive oil
4 large zucchini, sliced
1 cup white mushrooms, sliced
1 15-ounce can Italian-style stewed tomatoes
½ cup Italian-style bread crumbs
¼ cup shredded low-fat Parmesan cheese
¼ cup shredded low-fat mozzarella cheese

1. Coat a 9" × 13" baking dish with nonstick spray.

2. Place garlic and olive oil in a large skillet and sauté for 6 minutes on medium heat.

3. Add zucchini to skillet and sauté for 5 minutes. Add mushrooms to skillet and sauté for 5 minutes. Remove from burner, add tomatoes, and stir.

4. Pour veggies into the baking dish. Cover veggies with bread crumbs. Sprinkle both cheeses over bread crumbs.

5. Bake at 350°F for 15 minutes or until cheese melts and sauce boils.

Cheesy Cauliflower Bake

To add a bit of fun and color to this recipe, substitute broccoflower for cauliflower. Broccoflower has a similar taste and texture to cauliflower, but it's green.

1. In a large saucepan, bring cauliflower, ½ teaspoon salt, and water to a boil on medium-high heat. Cover saucepan and simmer 12 to 18 minutes or until cauliflower is tender. Drain cauliflower.

2. Mix Smart Squeeze, ½ teaspoon salt, black pepper, and cracker crumbs. Add cauliflower, onion, bell peppers, 1 cup Cheddar, and tomatoes to mixture and blend well.

3. Coat a 9" × 13" baking dish with nonstick spray. Add cauliflower mix to dish and bake uncovered at 350°F for 30 to 35 minutes.

4. Sprinkle remaining ½ cup cheese on top and bake for another 5 minutes.

Stadium Steps

If you live near a stadium of any sort, run, don't walk! Get the workout of your life by climbing stadium steps, which is a fantastic strength training workout for your entire lower body. It also happens to require a ton of endurance and burns gobs of calories.

Serves 6

234 calories
5g fat
39g carbohydrates
11g protein
847mg sodium
9g fiber

Ingredients

6 cups cauliflower, cut into chunks
1 teaspoon salt, divided
3 cups water
¼ cup Smart Squeeze
½ teaspoon ground black pepper
1 cup low-fat wheat crackers, crushed
1 white onion, chopped
½ cup bell peppers, chopped
1½ cups shredded low-fat Cheddar cheese
2 cups diced tomatoes

Cowboy Beans

Traditional baked beans are not such a healthy idea. This tasty recipe puts a healthy spin on an old favorite.

Serves 6

343 calories
6g fat
53g carbohydrates
26g protein
851mg sodium
11g fiber

Ingredients

1 pound 90 percent lean ground turkey
1 white onion, diced
1 bell pepper, diced
28 ounces vegetarian baked beans
14-ounce can kidney beans
½ cup mushrooms, sliced
¼ cup Splenda brown sugar
¾ cup low-sodium ketchup
1 teaspoon chili powder

1. Coat a skillet with nonstick spray. Brown turkey, onion, and pepper in skillet on medium-high heat until thoroughly cooked.

2. Add all ingredients to a slow cooker and cook for 3 to 4 hours.

Healthy Mushrooms

Mushrooms are high in fiber and protein and provide vitamins such as thiamine, riboflavin, and iron. Mushrooms provide a lot of other nutrients as well; they are particularly high in phosphorus and potassium.

Chapter 9
Dips, Spreads, and Dressings

Blueberry Sauce

Blueberry Sauce is a fabulous dessert topping. Try it over angel food cake, fat-free yogurt, muffins, or fat-free vanilla ice cream.

Combine orange juice, Splenda, and ginger in a medium saucepan. Bring to a boil and add blueberries. Cook for 1 minute and remove from stove. Cool before serving.

The Truth about Blueberries

Did you know blueberries are considered a superfood? Studies have shown them to improve balance, memory, and coordination, and they help you fight off things like cancer and cataracts! Sneak them into more than just fruit salads. Blueberries go great in yogurt, salads, smoothies, and desserts.

Serves 12

18 calories
0g fat
6g carbohydrates
0g protein
0mg sodium
1g fiber

Ingredients
½ cup orange juice
½ cup Splenda
1 teaspoon ground ginger
2 cups frozen blueberries, thawed

Spinach-Artichoke Dip

Serve this delicious dip with raw veggies, Pita Chips (page 126), or light whole grain Wasa crackers.

Thoroughly blend all ingredients in a food processor. Serve warm.

Yields 4 cups

177 calories
4g fat
13g carbohydrates
22g protein
1,011mg sodium
2g fiber

Ingredients
1 10-ounce package frozen spinach, thawed and drained
8-ounce can artichokes, drained
2 8-ounce packages fat-free cream cheese
1 clove fresh garlic, minced
3 tablespoons reduced-fat Parmesan cheese
½ teaspoon all-purpose seasoning

Black Bean Dip

To prevent the gas that often comes with the consumption of beans, add half a teaspoon of white vinegar to the bean mixture.

Thoroughly blend all ingredients in a food processor. Serve warm.

Serves 4

127 calories
1g fat
20g carbohydrates
10g protein
349mg sodium
6g fiber

Ingredients
14-ounce can black beans, drained
1 cup fat-free sour cream
¼ cup yellow onions, chopped
½ teaspoon fresh garlic, minced
1 tablespoon fresh cilantro, chopped
½ teaspoon jalapeño peppers

Simple Guacamole

Avocados are a unique fruit because they are naturally high in fat. Since you need some fat in your diet, guacamole makes a really healthy choice.

Mix all ingredients to desired texture.

Inspiration Is Everywhere
Fashion and fitness magazines offer up lean bodies for inspiration all the time. But can you find it elsewhere? The guy rolling around the gym in his wheelchair working out five days a week takes away your excuses. The mother of five training for a marathon might inspire you to make time. Seek out inspiration and use it to jumpstart your engine.

Serves 4

187 calories
15g fat
12g carbohydrates
4g protein
300mg sodium
3g fiber

Ingredients
2 ripe avocados, peeled and seeded
½ cup tomatoes, diced
½ teaspoon fresh garlic, minced
½ teaspoon salt
1 teaspoon green chili, finely minced
1 teaspoon freshly squeezed lemon juice
½ cup fat-free sour cream

Light Lemony Yogurt Sauce

This sauce is perfect to serve as a dip with fruit. You may even want to use it as a dressing over fruit salad.

Mix all ingredients together in a bowl and chill.

Friday Night Fitness
Instead of filling your Friday nights with cocktails and appetizers, fill it with music and dancing. Dancing is amazing exercise, and unlike group aerobics-style dance classes, you can dance for hours on end. So forget your sneakers, slap on a shiny shirt, and boogie on down.

Serves 6

27 calories
0g fat
5g carbohydrates
1g protein
20mg sodium
0g fiber

Ingredients
1 6-ounce container fat-free vanilla yogurt
1 tablespoon freshly squeezed lemon juice
1 teaspoon lemon rind, freshly grated
1 teaspoon mint leaves, finely chopped

Sweet Cocktail Sauce

Try out a variety of cocktail sauces with this recipe to see which you like best. Every brand has its own unique flavor, and it's worth the effort to find out which works best for you.

Combine all ingredients in a small bowl.

Serves 6

40 calories
0g fat
10g carbohydrates
1g protein
325mg sodium
1g fiber

Ingredients
1 cup cocktail sauce
2 tablespoons sugar-free orange marmalade
1 teaspoon ground ginger
¼ teaspoon fresh garlic, minced

Watermelon-Peach Salsa

Two cups of watermelon chunks are packed with nutrition. For only 80 calories, you'll get 30 percent of your recommended daily intake of vitamin A and 25 percent of vitamin C.

Combine all ingredients in a bowl and serve. To increase flavor, drizzle your favorite fat-free vinaigrette over the top.

Deviate from the Norm

For total body fitness, it's important to step off the beaten path once and a while. Do you normally pursue dance classes? Try basketball. New activities force your body to move in different ways, which creates new levels of strength, stamina, flexibility, and balance. Step outside your comfort zone and challenge that body once again.

Serves 6

41 calories
0g fat
10g carbohydrates
1g protein
1mg sodium
1g fiber

Ingredients

2 cups watermelon, chopped small
2 cups peaches, chopped small
1 tablespoon cilantro leaves, chopped
1 teaspoon hot pepper, diced

Black Olive Hummus

Hummus is a Middle Eastern spread commonly used with breads and vegetables. It is a high-protein alternative to meat.

Thoroughly blend all ingredients in a food processor.

Movie Theatre Snacks

Gobbling up obscene amounts of fat and calories has become a sad tradition in movie theaters. When you go to a movie, your best bet is to skip those snacks entirely. Except for an occasional soft pretzel, there are virtually zero healthy options at a theater. Smuggle in something healthy like dried fruit, baked chips, or veggie sticks, or choose to find satisfaction with two hours of entertainment.

Serves 4

130 calories
2g fat
23g carbohydrates
5g protein
371mg sodium
5g fiber

Ingredients
1 14-ounce can chickpeas
2 cloves garlic
¼ cup black olives, drained
Salt and pepper to taste

Lemon-Basil Hummus

This is a high-protein light snack that will go well with veggie sticks such as carrots, bell peppers, zucchini, broccoli, and cherry tomatoes.

Thoroughly blend all ingredients in a food processor.

Too Embarrassed to Work Out?
It's not uncommon to feel uncomfortable trying something new or doing something you're not already good at. But when it comes to fitness, as long as you show up and put forth your best effort, there's nothing to be embarrassed about! In fact, people tend to admire others who are exercising. Be proud and don't let fear hold you back!

Roasted Red Pepper Hummus

Not only does hummus serve as a great dipping spread, it's also ideal to stuff vegetables such as tomatoes, cucumbers, and zucchini.

Thoroughly blend all ingredients in a food processor.

Serves 4

122 calories
1g fat
24g carbohydrates
5g protein
297mg sodium
4g fiber

Ingredients
1 14-ounce can chickpeas
2 cloves garlic
1 teaspoon fresh basil, chopped
2 tablespoons freshly squeezed lemon juice

Serves 4

121 calories
1g fat
23g carbohydrates
5g protein
297mg sodium
4g fiber

Ingredients
1 14-ounce can chickpeas
2 cloves garlic
2 tablespoons roasted red peppers
Salt and pepper to taste

Low-Fat Alfredo Sauce

Alfredo sauce tends to burn easily if left unattended. Make sure you don't try to rush the sauce. Be patient, keep stirring, and keep a close eye on it.

Combine all ingredients in a large saucepan. Heat over medium-low heat and stir until smooth.

Alfredo = Big Bellies
Traditional Alfredo is the worst of all sauces. It's the perfect combination of butter, cream, and cheese, which leads to a caloric and fat count nightmare. If flat abs are on your to-do list, do not order this at a restaurant. Marinara will always be a better bet!

Serves 4

88 calories
1g fat
8g carbohydrates
12g protein
387mg sodium
0g fiber

Ingredients
*8-ounce package fat-free
    cream cheese*
*¼ cup reduced-fat Parmesan
    cheese*
¾ cup skim milk

Cranberry Surprise Spread

Chill this spread for at least 30 minutes before serving. The dip goes really well served with fruit, pita slices, or even the thinnest pretzel sticks.

Mix ingredients together in a bowl until they are thoroughly combined.

Serves 4

154 caloies
2g fat
17g carbohydrates
17g protein
631mg sodium
1g fiber

Ingredients

1 8-ounce package fat-free
  cream cheese
2 tablespoons frozen orange
  juice, thawed
1 tablespoon Splenda
1 tablespoon Spice Islands
  Orange Peel
1/8 teaspoon cinnamon
½ cup finely chopped dried
  cranberries

Fruit Dip

Serve this dip in the center of a fruit platter. It goes great with strawberries, bananas, pineapple, grapes, cantaloupe, and more.

Mix ingredients together in a bowl until thoroughly combined. Chill before serving.

Serves 4

62 calories
0g fat
12g carbohydrates
4g protein
38mg sodium
0g fiber

Ingredients

8 ounces fat-free sour cream
1½ tablespoons Splenda
  brown sugar
1 tablespoon Splenda
½ teaspoon cinnamon

Orangey Fruit Sauce

Serve this sauce as a dip for fruit or whole wheat crackers such as Wasa. You may even want to drizzle it over muffins or a cake you plan to serve immediately.

Mix ingredients together in a bowl until thoroughly combined. Chill before serving.

Serves 4

103 calories
0g fat
19g carbohydrates
7g protein
87mg sodium
0g fiber

Ingredients
16 ounces fat-free plain yogurt
2 tablespoons honey
1 tablespoon frozen orange juice concentrate
1 teaspoon grated orange zest

Cranberry BBQ Sauce

This sauce is superb as a feature in Chicken with Cranberry BBQ Sauce (page 187). It would also work well with turkey breast, beef, pork, veggies, and more.

Mix ingredients together in a bowl until thoroughly combined.

A Berry Old Tradition
Many American families make cranberry sauce for their Thanksgiving meals. This is not so much a coincidence as it is the true meaning of sticking with tradition. Cranberries were served at the original Thanksgiving dinner in 1621. Now dock your ship, don your petticoat, and give thanks!

Serves 6

110 calories
0g fat
28g carbohydrates
1g protein
87mg sodium
1g fiber

Ingredients
1 cup cranberry sauce
¼ cup sugar-free apricot preserves
2 tablespoons tomato paste
2 tablespoons balsamic vinegar
2 teaspoons yellow mustard
1 teaspoon chili powder
¼ teaspoon cumin

Spicy BBQ Sauce

Serves 4

24 calories
1g fat
4g carbohydrates
1g protein
270mg sodium
0g fiber

Ingredients
½ cup barbecue sauce
1 teaspoon Dijon mustard

Use this sauce on some of the wraps or pitas found in Chapter 3 or keep it on hand for cookouts. It's a flavorful way to update an old favorite.

Mix ingredients together in a bowl until thoroughly combined.

Fat-Free BBQ Ranch Dressing

Serves 8

28 calories
0g fat
5g carbohydrates
0g protein
277mg sodium
0g fiber

Ingredients
½ cup barbecue sauce
½ cup fat-free ranch dressing

Since the flavors of barbecue sauces and ranch dressings vary so greatly, you may want to try out a few different brands to find the combination that delights your taste buds the most!

Mix ingredients together in a bowl with a fork until thoroughly combined.

Fiesta Sauce

This sauce adds a spicy flair to any sandwich, salad, or wrap. Mix it up in 20 seconds flat and enjoy it with your favorites.

Mix ingredients together in a bowl with a fork until thoroughly combined.

Serves 8

33 calories
0g fat
6g carbohydrates
0g protein
303mg sodium
0g fiber

Ingredients
1 cup fat-free ranch dressing
1 teaspoon chili powder

Fat-Free Onion Dip

This dip is delicious and can be made in about 2 minutes flat. It's perfect for parties, and if you don't tell your guests it is fat-free, they'll never know!

Mix ingredients together in a bowl with a fork until thoroughly combined.

Serves 6

64 calories
0g fat
11g carbohydrates
6g protein
633mg sodium
1g fiber

Ingredients
16 ounces fat-free sour cream
*1 packet onion soup and dip
    mix*

Chips and Dip
A constant staple at social gatherings, chips and dip no longer has to be a source of weight gain. You can find a wide variety of chips in baked versions in grocery stores everywhere. These are a much healthier alternative to the fried versions. Fat-free sour cream and cream cheese make a strong foundation for any dip.

Berbere African Spice

33 calories
1g fat
8g carbohydrates
1g protein
540mg sodium
3g fiber

Ingredients

2 tablespoons ground red
   pepper
1 tablespoon black pepper
¼ teaspoon ground cloves
1 teaspoon ground cinnamon
1 teaspoon ground ginger
¼ teaspoon salt

Pronounced "ber-beray," berbere is a spice mixture commonly used in Ethiopia. It's commonly used as a spice or rub for both white and red meats.

Combine all ingredients in a bowl.

Moving Meetings

Plan casual get-togethers or meetings with people you know fairly well with fitness in mind. Treadmills, steppers, or nearby trails offer the ideal opportunity for busy people to kill two birds with one stone. An hour of interrupted conversation combined with a stress-busting workout may be just what you need to seal the deal.

Ginger Dressing

This dressing is quite versatile. Serve it alongside sweet salads, vegetables, and meats. It's delicious!

Combine all ingredients in a closed container and shake until well blended.

Tales of the Tape

You're striving to create a flatter belly, so just like any other effort you make, you should keep tabs on your progress! Make a habit of wrapping some measuring tape around your waist and keeping notes. Waistbands can be deceiving, so play statistician and measure your success with actual measurements!

Yields 1 cup

11 calories
0g fat
2g carbohydrates
0g protein
50mg sodium
0g fiber

Ingredients
2/3 cup pineapple juice
1 tablespoon low sodium soy sauce
1 teaspoon fresh ginger, grated
1 tablespoon Splenda
2 tablespoons cider vinegar
½ teaspoon sesame oil

Chapter 10
Pizza

Cheese Pizza

When looking for the perfect marinara sauce, be open to various brands and flavors. Choose sauces that are low in fat, but taste test everything you can find that fits that criterion.

1. Top pita with marinara, mozzarella, and basil.
2. Cook at 350°F for 6 to 8 minutes or until cheese has melted.

Microwavable Options

Any of these personal pizzas can be made in the microwave. Simply make your pizza and put it in the microwave for 45 to 60 seconds or until the cheese has melted. In addition, you can use light-wheat English muffins instead of pitas. Toast each English muffin half, add your toppings, and put your pizza in the microwave for 20 to 30 seconds to melt the cheese.

Serves 2

115 calories
1g fat
20g carbohydrates
8g protein
346mg sodium
3g fiber

Ingredients

1 large whole wheat pita
2 tablespoons marinara sauce
¼ cup shredded fat-free mozzarella cheese
½ teaspoon basil

White Pizza

White pizzas rely more on cheese for flavor than do their traditional counterparts. Experiment with different low-fat cheeses, fresh herbs, and garlic.

1. Top pita with ricotta, mozzarella, and salt.

2. Cook at 350°F for 6 to 8 minutes or until cheese has melted.

Training Tips from Jane and John
To learn a bunch of new exercises, ask your friends what type of things they do to stay fit. Maybe Jane has some fun abdominal training techniques to share, and John can show you how he gets his shoulders looking so strong. Trainers are terrific, but you'd be surprised by the cool things your friends and neighbors can do!

Serves 2

117 calories
1g fat
19g carbohydrates
10g protein
312g sodium
2g fiber

Ingredients
1 large whole wheat pita
2 tablespoons fat-free ricotta cheese
¼ cup shredded fat-free mozzarella cheese
Dash of salt to taste

Breakfast Pizza

This is the perfect breakfast or lunch for someone looking for lots of flavor on little effort. It's so simple, little kids can make it.

Serves 1

138 calories
2g fat
25g carbohydrates
12g protein
450mg sodium
9g fiber

Ingredients
1 light-wheat English muffin, split
2 tablespoons marinara sauce
2 tablespoons shredded fat-free mozzarella cheese

1. Toast English muffin halves in toaster.

2. Place toasted muffin on paper plate.

3. Top each half with 1 tablespoon marinara topped with 1 tablespoon mozzarella.

4. Cook in microwave for 20 to 30 seconds or until cheese has melted.

Suck It in, Soldier!

Standing like a slouch conditions your abdominal muscles to hang loose, which looks unflattering. Instead, stand up tall with shoulders back and pull your belly button in toward your spinal cord. Pretend you're strutting around in a bikini all day and your abdominal muscles will learn this tighter posture, leading to a flatter look.

Barbecue Pizza

This recipe is proof that you can enjoy your favorite flavors without paying a painful physical price.

1. Shred chicken breasts.

2. Top pita with barbecue sauce, chicken, mozzarella, salt, and pepper.

3. In oven, cook at 350°F for 6 to 8 minutes or until cheese has melted

Serves 2

212 calories
1g fat
33g carbohydrates
14g protein
301mg sodium
2g fiber

Ingredients
½ Simply Grilled Chicken Breast recipe (page 176), cooked
1 large whole wheat pita
2 tablespoons sweet barbecue sauce
¼ cup shredded fat-free mozzarella cheese
Dash of salt and pepper

Buffalo Pizza

The combination of crispy chicken, wing sauce, and cheese makes for a wildly flavorful and textured pizza. Make it for football parties!

1. Top pita with sauce, chicken, and mozzarella in that order.

2. In oven, cook at 350°F for 6 to 8 minutes or until cheese has melted.

Serves 2

170 calories
2g fat
23g carbohydrates
17g protein
471mg sodium
3g fiber

Ingredients
1 large whole wheat pita
2 tablespoons Crystal Wing Sauce
½ breast of Oven "Fried" Southern Chicken (page 40), cooked and chopped
1 ounce shredded fat-free mozzarella cheese

Eggplant Pizza

The combination of eggplant and tomatoes is a lycopene dream. Lycopene is great for both your heart and your vision.

Serves 2

138 calories
4g fat
21g carbohydrates
8g protein
429mg sodium
3g fiber

Ingredients
1 large whole wheat pita
2 tablespoons marinara sauce
¼ cup eggplant, peeled and diced
1 tablespoon sun-dried tomatoes, chopped
2 tablespoons shredded fat-free mozzarella cheese
1 tablespoon Gorgonzola cheese

1. Top pita with marinara, eggplant, tomatoes, mozzarella, and Gorgonzola.

2. In oven, cook at 350°F for 6 to 8 minutes or until cheese has melted.

Ballpark Strategy

Never plan to eat a meal at a sporting event. Ballparks are synonymous with garbage food, and it's a bad idea to be stuck there starving while surrounded by lukewarm pizzas, hotdogs, and nachos. Instead, eat a healthy meal before you go. If you must have a snack, stick to a soft pretzel or a sorbet.

Spinach Pizza

Just like it did for Popeye, spinach will make you strong. It's full of iron, vitamin A, and fiber, which is helpful in blood cell production and brain cell development.

1. Top pita with mozzarella, feta, spinach, tomatoes, and garlic.

2. In oven, cook at 350°F for 6 to 8 minutes or until cheese has melted.

Pizza History
Pizza was created in Naples around the third century B.C. Ancient scholars recorded its origins as a flat round of dough dressed with olive oil, herbs, and honey. Other writings describe a sheet of flour filled with cheese and honey, flavored with bay leaves.

Serves 2

118 calories
2g fat
19g carbohydrates
8g protein
313mg sodium
3g fiber

Ingredients
1 large whole wheat pita
3 tablespoons shredded fat-free mozzarella cheese
1 tablespoon feta cheese
½ cup fresh spinach, chopped
2 tablespoons Roma tomatoes, chopped
½ teaspoon fresh garlic, minced

Yankee Pizza

The full-fat pizza dough version of this recipe includes gobs of fat and calories.

1. Top pita with mozzarella, ricotta, tomatoes, and garlic.

2. In oven, cook at 350°F for 6 to 8 minutes or until cheese has melted.

Serves 2

110 calories
1g fat
19g carbohydrates
8g protein
257mg sodium
3g fiber

Ingredients
1 large whole wheat pita
2 tablespoons shredded fat-free mozzarella cheese
2 tablespoons fat-free ricotta cheese
2 tablespoons Roma tomatoes
½ teaspoon fresh garlic, minced

Hawaiian Pizza

Try using coconut flakes to make this pizza feel more Hawaiian.

1. Top pita with marinara, mozzarella, bacon, and pineapples.

2. In oven, cook at 350°F for 6 to 8 minutes or until cheese has melted.

Serves 2

168 calories
3g fat
22g carbohydrates
14g protein
746mg sodium
3g fiber

Ingredients
1 large whole wheat pita
2 tablespoons marinara sauce
¼ cup shredded fat-free mozzarella cheese
2 ounces (2 thin slices) low-sodium Canadian bacon, in chunks
2 tablespoons pineapple, in small chunks

Good, Bad, and Thin
Pizza has the potential to be really good or really bad for you. The power is in your hands. When making or ordering pizza, make sure you always choose the thinnest crust possible while piling on lean meats and fresh or grilled produce. Another great idea is to go light on the cheese.

Fitz's Thanksgiving Pizza

This unique spin on pizza is quick, sweet, and delicious. The skin on the potato is the most nutritious, so leave it on; it enhances the textures as well.

1. Bake sweet potato with skin on in microwave for 10 to 12 minutes, or until soft. On a plate, mash potato with fork.

2. Place pita on a plate and smear sweet potato to cover it. Dash with salt. Top potato with gravy, followed by turkey.

3. Cook at 350°F for 6 to 8 minutes or microwave for 45 to 60 seconds.

Serves 2

205 calories
3g fat
34g carbohydrates
12g protein
223mg sodium
4g fiber

Ingredients

1 whole wheat pita
1 medium sweet potato
1 tablespoon fat-free turkey gravy
2 ounces roasted turkey breast, cut in small chunks
Dash of salt

Spinach and Mushroom Pizza

This gloriously low-calorie pizza is a great way to get your greens.

Top pita with marinara, mozzarella, spinach, and mushrooms. Cook at 350°F for 6 to 8 minutes, or until cheese has melted.

Serves 2

130 calories
1g fat
22g carbohydrates
10g protein
379mg sodium
4g fiber

Ingredients

1 large whole wheat pita
2 tablespoons marinara sauce
¼ cup shredded fat-free mozzarella cheese
8 fresh spinach leaves
3 white mushrooms, sliced

Veggie Galore Pizza

Serves 2

117 calories
1g fat
20g carbohydrates
8g protein
347mg sodium
3g fiber

Ingredients

1 large whole wheat pita
2 tablespoons marinara
    sauce
¼ cup shredded fat-free
    mozzarella cheese
½ teaspoon fresh basil,
    chopped
1 teaspoon bell peppers,
    diced
1 teaspoon white onions,
    diced
1 tablespoon broccoli florets,
    chopped
1 tablespoon tomato, diced

This pie is perfect for a friendly, healthy get-together. Vary the veggies on the pizza according to your tastes and what you have in the refrigerator.

1. Spray a small pan with nonstick spray and bake peppers, onions, and broccoli in oven at 350°F for 6 minutes.

2. Top pita with marinara, mozzarella, basil, baked veggies, and tomatoes. Cook at 350°F for 6 to 8 minutes, or until cheese has melted, or microwave for 45 to 60 seconds, or until cheese has melted.

Chapter 11
Poultry

Simply Grilled Chicken Breasts

Grill more chicken than you can eat when you make this recipe. Seal the leftovers in plastic containers; they're perfect to use in salads and soups throughout your week.

Serves 6

130 calories
1g fat
0g carbohydrates
27g protein
97mg sodium
0g fiber

Ingredients
*6 boneless, skinless chicken
    breasts
½ teaspoon all-purpose
    seasoning*

1. Trim visible fat from chicken breasts.

2. Sprinkle chicken with all-purpose seasoning.

3. Coat skillet with nonstick spray.

4. Place chicken in skillet and cook on medium heat for 12 to 15 minutes or until internal temperature of chicken is 165°F or juices run clear when pricked.

Frozen Is Fine
Don't feel pressured to purchase fresh meat daily. Hit the frozen food section and buy a large bag of your favorite grilled meat. It's just as good and will last in your freezer for months, and you'll always have a healthy option for spontaneous meals.

Sweet Crusted Chicken Nuggets

This recipe may surprise you and everyone you serve it to. Sweet chicken sounds strange, but it is guaranteed to please.

1. Preheat oven to 400°F.

2. Coat chicken chunks in Egg Beaters.

3. Roll coated chicken in frosted flakes until covered.

4. Place chicken on two large cookie sheets and sprinkle with Splenda.

5. Bake for 20 minutes or until internal temperature reaches 165°F.

Serves 4

360 calories
2g fat
55g carbohydrates
32g protein
392mg sodium
1g fiber

Ingredients
4 boneless, skinless chicken breasts, trimmed of fat and cut into chunks
1 cup Egg Beaters
2 cups frosted flakes cereal
1 tablespoon Splenda

Island Fajitas

Serves 4

303 calories
4g fat
38g carbohydrates
30g protein
544mg sodium
4g fiber

Ingredients

½ cup canned pineapple juice
¾ pound boneless, skinless
    chicken breast, sliced
1 bell pepper, sliced
1 large red onion, sliced
½ cup white mushrooms,
    sliced
4 whole wheat tortillas
1 cup iceberg lettuce,
    shredded
1 cup diced tomatoes
½ cup shredded fat-free
    Cheddar cheese

Try varying the types of vegetables you use in this recipe. Mix in corn, squash, broccoli, peas, or anything else you find interesting.

1. Pour pineapple juice over chicken strips in a glass dish. Cover and marinate in the refrigerator for 30 minutes.

2. Drain marinade and broil chicken with peppers, onions, and mushrooms until meat is fully cooked and veggies are tender.

3. Evenly divide and place all ingredients into tortillas. Top with lettuce, tomatoes, and cheese and roll them up.

Tuscan Chicken and Sun-Dried Tomatoes

If you use a dry herb instead of a fresh herb, halve the amount. For example, 1 teaspoon of dried basil is equivalent to 2 teaspoons of fresh basil.

1. Spray a 9" × 13" baking dish with cooking spray. Lay chicken in the dish, leaving some space between each piece.

2. Mix remaining ingredients in a separate bowl. Pour mixture over chicken and cover with foil.

3. Bake at 375°F for 45 minutes.

Cooking Chicken
When making chicken, you should cook it until the internal temperature reaches 165°F. You can eyeball the status of your meal by cutting into the thickest part of the chicken breast and checking for pink. If any of the meat has a pinkish tinge, put it back in the oven. Ensure your meat is totally white before you take a bite.

Serves 6

192 calories
3g fat
4g carbohydrates
30g protein
297mg sodium
1g fiber

Ingredients
6 boneless, skinless chicken breasts
½ tablespoon olive oil
1 clove fresh garlic, minced
½ teaspoon all-purpose seasoning
½ cup red wine
1 cup low-sodium chicken broth
1 teaspoon dried basil or 2 teaspoons fresh basil
½ cup sun-dried tomatoes, sliced
½ cup yellow onions, sliced

Chicken Breasts with Rosemary

Serves 6

177 calories
3g fat
3g carbohydrates
28g protein
125mg sodium
0g fiber

Ingredients

6 boneless, skinless chicken
    breasts
½ tablespoon olive oil
1 clove fresh garlic, minced
½ teaspoon all-purpose
    seasoning
2 teaspoons balsamic vinegar
2 tablespoons lemon juice
1 cup red cooking wine
1 teaspoon rosemary
1 cup tomatoes, diced
¼ teaspoon black pepper

According to ancient Greeks, rosemary was believed to enhance intelligence and memory. It wasn't uncommon to see Greek students wearing this spice in their hair to help them excel in school.

1. Coat a large skillet with nonstick spray. Place chicken on skillet, being careful not to crowd the meat.

2. In a separate bowl, mix remaining ingredients. Pour mixture over chicken.

3. Cook on medium high for 10 to 12 minutes, turn chicken, and simmer for 8 minutes.

Baked Chicken with Vegetables

Feel free to use a frozen bag of the mixed vegetables instead of preparing fresh veggies.

1. Spray a 9" × 13" baking dish with nonstick spray. Place the chicken in the dish, being careful not to crowd the meat.

2. In a separate bowl, mix remaining ingredients. Pour mixture over chicken, cover with foil.

3. Bake at 380°F for 45 minutes.

Rules for Eating Out

Never order meat that has been fried or sautéed, and always request that it be cooked without oil or butter for assurance. Do the same for your veggies, although it's great to eat them raw. Keep bread baskets off the table; you don't need that! Request all sauces and dressings on the side.

Serves 6

197 calories
3g fat
10g carbohydrates
30g protein
454mg sodium
5g fiber

Ingredients
6 boneless, skinless chicken
    breasts
3 cups mixed vegetables
1 cup white mushrooms,
    sliced
1 cup celery, sliced
1 cup onion chunks
2 teaspoons olive oil
1 teaspoon all-purpose
    seasoning
½ teaspoon fresh garlic,
    minced
½ cup water
½ cup chicken broth
½ teaspoon red pepper flakes
½ teaspoon dried basil
½ teaspoon parsley

Coq au Vin

Serves 6

309 calories
6g fat
23g carbohydrates
33g protein
498mg sodium
3g fiber

Ingredients

6 boneless, skinless chicken
    breasts, cut in chunks
½ teaspoon olive oil
1 clove fresh garlic, minced
½ teaspoon all-purpose
    seasoning
1 cup red wine
1 cup chicken broth
1 cup onions, chopped
1 cup carrots, sliced
1½ teaspoons dried thyme
1 teaspoon dried rosemary
1 teaspoon black pepper
½ cup turkey bacon, sliced
½ cup pitted prunes
3 bay leaves
½ cup flour

Prunes are dried plums, and they should be left whole in this recipe. They're sweet, chewy, and have a productive effect on the digestive system.

1. Spray a 9" × 13" baking dish with nonstick spray. Place chicken in dish.

2. In a separate bowl, mix remaining ingredients. Pour mixture over chicken and cover with foil.

3. Bake at 360°F for 45 minutes or until thoroughly cooked and sauce thickens.

Did You Know?
Coq au vin is a traditional French dish made of chicken pieces stewed in red wine. Its original purpose was for tenderizing tough, old fowl. Do not use an aluminum pot when making it because it will react with the wine and turn your chicken purple!

Chicken with Lime Sauce

Limes and lemons need to be washed well before slicing to prevent E. coli infections. Run them under water and scrub the peel with a produce scrub brush.

1. Spray a 9" × 13" baking dish with nonstick spray. Place chicken in the dish, being careful not to crowd the meat.

2. In a separate bowl, mix remaining ingredients. Pour mixture over chicken and cover with foil.

3. Bake at 380°F for 45 minutes.

Serves 6

174 calories
3g fat
7g carbohydrates
29g protein
249mg sodium
1g fiber

Ingredients
6 boneless, skinless chicken breasts
½ tablespoon olive oil
1 clove fresh garlic, minced
½ teaspoon all-purpose seasoning
1 cup chicken broth
1½ tablespoons brown sugar
¼ cup lemon juice
2 teaspoons mustard
3 tablespoons water
1 teaspoon cornstarch
1 cup yellow onions, sliced
1½ tablespoons Smart Squeeze
½ cup limes, sliced
¼ cup parsley

Thai Chicken Sauté

Serves 6

224 calories
8g fat
10g carbohydrates
28g protein
255mg sodium
1g fiber

Ingredients

½ tablespoon olive oil
1 clove fresh garlic, minced
6 boneless, skinless chicken
    breasts, cut in chunks
½ teaspoon all-purpose
    seasoning
2 tablespoons cornstarch
1 teaspoon ground ginger
2 tablespoons hoisin sauce
½ cup coconut milk
1 tablespoon hot sauce
1 tablespoon sugar or
    Splenda
1 tablespoon lemon juice
1 cup onions, sliced
3 tablespoons cilantro

Thai food traditionally combines a variety of sweet and fiery flavors. This particular dish combines the sweetness of coconut milk with the spice of hot sauce.

1. Heat olive oil in a large skillet over medium heat. Sauté garlic for 1 to 2 minutes until garlic is fragrant but not brown.

2. Add chicken to skillet and sauté for 5 minutes.

3. In a separate bowl, mix all-purpose seasoning, cornstarch, ginger, hoisin sauce, coconut milk, hot sauce, sugar, and lemon juice. Blend well.

4. Add mixture to chicken. Cook for 10 minutes.

5. Add onions and cilantro and simmer for 8 to 10 minutes or until sauce thickens.

Spicy Honey-Brushed Chicken Breast

This dish is delightful grilled. Just grill chicken first and then brush with honey sauce. The sauce is fabulous over baked salmon as well.

1. Mix all ingredients except chicken in a large bowl. Add chicken to mixture and coat each breast well on each side.

2. Spray a skillet with nonstick spray. Add chicken to skillet and cook over medium heat for 6 to 8 minutes on each side.

Whole Grains
Whole grain bread, pasta, and crackers are ideal because they have plenty of fiber and nutrients; refined grains do not. Whole grain products are made with the entire grain kernel and serve as a tremendous source of energy for your body. Besides fiber, they're also loaded with B vitamins and iron. Choose whole grains over white products every time.

Serves 6

233 calories
3g fat
25g carbohydrates
28g protein
112mg sodium
1g fiber

Ingredients
½ tablespoon olive oil
1 clove fresh garlic, minced
½ teaspoon all-purpose seasoning
3 teaspoons chili powder
1 teaspoon cumin
1 teaspoon paprika
½ teaspoon red pepper
½ cup honey
1 tablespoon cider vinegar
6 boneless, skinless chicken breasts

Spanish Chicken Fricassee

Serves 6

208 calories
3g fat
12g carbohydrates
29g protein
256mg sodium
2g fiber

Ingredients

1½ pounds boneless, skinless
   chicken breasts, cut in
   large chunks
½ tablespoon olive oil
1 clove fresh garlic, minced
½ teaspoon all-purpose
   seasoning
2 teaspoons paprika
1 teaspoon black pepper
½ cup bell peppers, diced
½ cup white onions, diced
½ cup celery, sliced
1 cup chicken broth
½ cup wine
1 cup carrots, sliced
1 cup tomatoes, diced
2 tablespoons parsley
3 bay leaves
1 cup Yukon potatoes, cubed

Fricassees are Spanish stews that typically involve some sort of poultry, although other types of white meat can be used. Its base is usually created with wine or dry vermouth.

1. Add all ingredients except potatoes to large saucepan. Cook on medium high for 10 minutes, stirring often.

2. Add potatoes and simmer for another 15 minutes or until sauce thickens, stirring occasionally.

Chafing

If irritating and painful chafing has been keeping you from running the miles or climbing the steps you want to, your problem has a simple solution. Both petroleum jelly and a product called BodyGlide are extremely effective in preventing and relieving chafing. Just slide some on your problem areas and go!

Salt-Crusted Herbed Chicken

Kosher salt or sea salt is used to coat chicken or steak to preserve the natural juices of the meat while it's being grilled.

1. Mix garlic, pepper, lemon juice, oregano, thyme, and water in a bowl. Coat chicken in mixture and lay on a tray. Sprinkle both sides of the chicken with kosher salt.

2. Grill chicken for 5 to 6 minutes on each side. Remove chicken from grill with tongs and smack it against the grill to remove excess salt.

Serves 6

137 calories
2g fat
2g carbohydrates
27g protein
1,017mg sodium
1g fiber

Ingredients
1 clove fresh garlic, minced
¼ teaspoon black pepper
¼ cup lemon juice
1 tablespoon oregano
1 tablespoon thyme
1 tablespoon water
6 boneless, skinless chicken breasts
1 tablespoon kosher salt

Chicken with Cranberry BBQ Sauce

This is a great Thanksgiving option for folks who don't enjoy turkey! To make this recipe on the grill, grill the chicken first and then add sauce toward the end.

1. Spray a 9" × 13" baking dish with nonstick spray. Place the chicken in the dish, being careful not to crowd the meat.

2. In a separate bowl, mix the remaining ingredients. Pour the mixture over chicken and cover with foil.

3. Bake at 375°F for 45 minutes or until thoroughly cooked.

Serves 6

260 calories
4g fat
28g carbohydrates
28g protein
174mg sodium
1g fiber

Ingredients
6 boneless, skinless chicken breasts
1 clove fresh garlic, minced
½ teaspoon all-purpose seasoning
1 tablespoon olive oil
½ teaspoon coriander
1 cup Cranberry BBQ Sauce (page 159)

Kung Pao Chicken

Serves 6

258 calories
9g fat
11g carbohydrates
34g protein
650mg sodium
3g fiber

Ingredients

6 boneless, skinless chicken
    breasts, cut in strips
4 cups broccoli florets
1 teaspoon sesame oil
1 clove fresh garlic, minced
½ teaspoon all-purpose
    seasoning
2 tablespoons ground ginger
1 teaspoon crushed red
    pepper
1 cup chicken broth
1 cup water
3 tablespoons hoisin sauce
3 tablespoons rice wine
    vinegar
3 tablespoons low-sodium
    soy sauce
¼ cup peanuts
1 teaspoon cornstarch

The kung pao chicken found in shopping malls around the world is high in fat because it uses cheap dark meat chicken and is fried. This meal provides the flavor without the fat.

1. Mix all ingredients in a large bowl.

2. Spray skillet with nonstick spray. Add chicken mixture to skillet. Cook on medium high for 10 to 15 minutes, stirring often.

Secret Sugar

There are many ways to disguise the word "sugar" on a food label. Here's a big list for you to remember so you're not fooled in the future: high fructose corn syrup, fruit juice concentrate, sucrose, glucose, dextrose, honey, molasses, brown sugar, corn sweetener, corn syrup, fructose, and invert sugar.

Hungarian Chicken Paprikas

Paprikas is a Hungarian dish made with diced meat and covered with a sauce made with paprika.

1. Spray skillet with nonstick spray. Add olive oil, garlic, and chicken chunks to skillet. Sauté on medium high for 5 minutes, stirring often.

2. Add remaining ingredients except sour cream to skillet. Cook for 5 minutes.

3. Add sour cream, stirring well, and simmer for 5 to 8 minutes.

Serves 6

202 calories
3g fat
11g carbohydrates
32g protein
343mg sodium
2g fiber

Ingredients

½ tablespoon olive oil
1 clove fresh garlic, minced
6 boneless, skinless chicken
    breasts, cut in chunks
½ teaspoon all-purpose
    seasoning
1 cup bell peppers, diced
1 cup white onions, diced
1 cup chicken broth
1 tablespoon paprika
½ teaspoon chili powder
¼ cup tomato paste
1 cup fat-free sour cream

Spicy Curry Sesame Chicken

Sesame seeds are oil-rich ingredients that add a nutty flavor as well as healthy sesame oil to your recipes.

1. Spray large skillet with nonstick spray.

2. Mix all ingredients in a large bowl. Pour mixture into skillet. Cook on medium high for 10 to 12 minutes, stirring often. Simmer for 5 to 10 minutes.

Avoid the Crash and Burn
Food is fuel for your body, but some food won't fill your tank as it should. Instead of making you feel strong and energetic, sugary junk foods will leave you feeling sluggish and grouchy. You'll also have less room and desire for the healthy food that your body truly needs to be its best.

Serves 6

169 calories
4g fat
3g carbohydrates
28g protein
286mg sodium
1g fiber

Ingredients
6 boneless, skinless chicken breasts, cut in chunks
½ cup chicken broth
1 teaspoon cornstarch
1 tablespoon curry powder
½ teaspoon all-purpose seasoning
1 clove fresh garlic, minced
1 teaspoon sesame seeds
1 cup sliced yellow onions
1 tablespoon olive oil
2 tablespoons hot sauce

Drunken Philippine Chicken

Lemon flavors are quite popular in Philippine cuisine. If you make any other recipes that require you to use juice, go for the sugar-free version; this recipe uses Crystal Light.

1. Spray a 9" × 13" baking dish with nonstick spray. Place the chicken in the dish, being careful not to crowd the meat.

2. In a separate bowl, mix the remaining ingredients. Pour mixture over the chicken and cover with foil.

3. Bake at 380°F for 45 minutes.

Fruit Versus Fruit Juice
It's absolutely better to eat whole fruit than drink juice. Fruit juice often has some of the nutrients found in fruit, but it loses most of the fiber. Juice is often loaded with sugar and will never fill you up like chewing on actual food will! Stick with calorie-free beverages and make real produce a daily part of your diet.

Serves 6

173 calories
2g fat
10g carbohydrates
30g protein
126mg sodium
0g fiber

Ingredients
6 boneless, skinless chicken breasts
1 cup Crystal Light lemonade
½ cup low-sodium ketchup
1 clove fresh garlic, minced
½ teaspoon all-purpose seasoning
1 tablespoon Worcestershire sauce
2 tablespoons gin
1 teaspoon olive oil
1 tablespoon green chilies, finely chopped

Crispy Chicken Tenders

Chicken tenders do not always have to be fried and full of fat. If you want the taste of fried chicken without adding to your waist, make your own!

1. Spray a 9" × 13" baking dish with nonstick spray.

2. In a large bowl, mix chicken strips and egg substitute together.

3. In a separate bowl, mix remaining ingredients.

4. Dip chicken tenders into dry mixture, coating completely.

5. Place chicken on baking dish and bake uncovered at 370°F for 40 minutes, turning once.

Serves 6

262 calories
9g fat
7g carbohydrates
36g protein
781mg sodium
0g fiber

Ingredients

6 boneless, skinless chicken breasts, cut into strips
¼ cup Egg Beaters
1 cup grated reduced-fat Parmesan cheese
½ teaspoon thyme
1 teaspoon all-purpose seasoning
1 clove fresh garlic, minced
1½ cups crispy rice cereal

Spicy Barbecue Chicken

If you order barbecue chicken at a restaurant, be sure to request white meat only. Once your meal arrives, remove the skin before you dig in.

1. Mix bread crumbs, garlic, and all-purpose seasoning in a bowl.

2. Coat chicken breasts in Spicy BBQ Sauce. Dip chicken into bread crumb mixture, coating well.

3. Coat a 9" × 13" baking dish with nonstick spray. Place the chicken in the dish, being careful not to crowd the meat.

4. Bake uncovered at 350°F for 40 minutes, turning chicken once.

Serves 6

218 calories
3g fat
16g carbohydrates
30g protein
432mg sodium
1g fiber

Ingredients

1 cup bread crumbs
1 clove fresh garlic, minced
½ teaspoon all-purpose seasoning
6 boneless, skinless chicken breasts
Spicy BBQ Sauce (page 160)

Orange Chicken Paradise

No need to concern yourself with the alcohol in this recipe; the brandy burns away in the cooking process.

1. Spray a 9" × 13" baking dish with nonstick spray. Place the chicken in the dish, being careful not to crowd the meat.

2. In a separate bowl, mix remaining ingredients. Pour mixture over chicken and cover with foil.

3. Bake at 370°F for 45 minutes.

Serves 6

234 calories
5g fat
15g carbohydrates
29g protein
106mg sodium
2g fiber

Ingredients

6 boneless, skinless chicken breasts
½ tablespoon olive oil
1 clove fresh garlic, minced
½ teaspoon all-purpose seasoning
1 cup orange slices
½ cup yellow onions, in large chunks
1 cup carrots, sliced
1 cup orange juice
2 tablespoons brandy
3 tablespoons sesame seeds
2 tablespoons cornstarch

Aunt Kathy's Asian Roasted Chicken

Roasting the soy sauce, brown sugar, and sesame oil will create a caramelizing effect on the chicken. This will give the chicken a brown color and an intense flavor.

1. Spray a 9" × 13" baking dish with nonstick spray. Place the chicken in the dish, being careful not to crowd the meat.

2. In a separate bowl, mix remaining ingredients. Pour mixture over chicken.

3. Bake uncovered at 350°F for 45 minutes.

Indian Treasure Tandoori Chicken

Turmeric is a spice that belongs to the ginger family, and it's one of the main ingredients in Asian curries.

1. Coat large skillet with nonstick spray. Add chicken, olive oil, and garlic to skillet. Sauté for 5 to 8 minutes on medium high, stirring often.

2. Add remaining ingredients except for sour cream to skillet and stir. Cook on medium heat for 8 to 10 minutes.

3. Add sour cream and mix well. Simmer and stir for another 5 minutes.

The Danger in Drinking
Even one alcoholic beverage can sabotage your fitness efforts for the evening. People who allow themselves one drink are more likely to have another drink, consume food they normally wouldn't, and skip their workouts the next day. It's just not worth it. Avoid even one drink and save yourself tons of calories!

Serves 6

286 calories
4g fat
3g carbohydrates
56g protein
184mg sodium
0g fiber

Ingredients
6 boneless, skinless chicken breasts, cut in chunks
½ tablespoon olive oil
1 clove fresh garlic, minced
¼ cup yellow onions, sliced
½ teaspoon ground ginger
½ teaspoon coriander
½ teaspoon all-purpose seasoning
¼ teaspoon cumin
¼ teaspoon turmeric
¼ teaspoon red pepper
¼ teaspoon black pepper
1 cup tomatoes, diced
¼ cup fat-free sour cream

Tropical Jerk Chicken

Serves 6

151 calories
2g fat
3g carbohydrates
28g protein
99mg sodium
1g fiber

Ingredients

¼ cup yellow onions, coarsely chopped
¼ cup green onions, coarsely chopped
¼ cup white onions, coarsely chopped
1 clove fresh garlic, minced
2 tablespoons cider vinegar
2 teaspoons brown sugar
1 teaspoon thyme
1 teaspoon allspice
1 teaspoon olive oil
½ teaspoon nutmeg
1 teaspoon jalapeño pepper
½ teaspoon all-purpose seasoning
6 boneless, skinless chicken breasts

Jerk is a style of cooking, popular in Jamaica, that combines a variety of onions with spices to create a rub. This is a very healthy and low-calorie way to flavor your food.

1. Add the three types of coarsely chopped onions in a food processor and mix ten seconds until blended together.

2. In a bowl, add onion mixture and remaining ingredients except for chicken. Mix well.

3. Coat each chicken breast with mixture.

4. Place chicken on grill and cook for 6 minutes on each side.

Turkey Lasagna

To drop the calorie count on this recipe even further, remove the lasagna noodles completely and blend these ingredients as a casserole.

Serves 10 to 12

315 calories
6g fat
29g carbohydrates
36g protein
885mg sodium
3g fiber

Ingredients
*1 8-ounce box cooked
    lasagna pasta
1 large zucchini, sliced
1 large squash, sliced
1 cup broccoli florets
1 pound 90 percent lean
    ground turkey
3 cups marinara sauce
1¾ cups fat-free ricotta
    cheese
¼ cup Egg Beaters, slightly
    beaten
½ teaspoon dried basil
½ teaspoon oregano
16 ounces (2 cups) fat-free
    shredded mozzarella
    cheese
¼ cup reduced-fat Parmesan
    cheese*

1. Boil lasagna pasta until softened.

2. Cook veggies in nonstick pan on medium heat until they start to brown. Remove veggies from heat and set aside. Cook turkey over medium heat until browned.

3. Drain the turkey and stir in marinara sauce.

4. In small bowl, stir together ricotta, Egg Beaters, basil, and oregano.

5. Spread ¾ cup of turkey and marinara sauce mixture in 13" × 9" × 2" baking dish.

6. Place three pieces of lasagna noodles crosswise over sauce. Spread ⅔ cup ricotta mixture, then ¾ cup turkey sauce, then ½ cup veggies evenly over pasta. Sprinkle with 1 cup mozzarella and Parmesan cheese. Repeat with remaining ingredients.

7. Cover with foil and bake for 30 minutes. Remove foil. Bake 10 to 15 minutes more until bubbly.

TV Toy Bin
Television time doesn't have to be a bad thing, as long as you're not sitting in front of the TV while you should be working out. Instead, do both! Fill a basket with weights, resistance bands, a yoga mat, and a jump rope and place it near your flat screen. Instead of loafing while you watch your favorite show, lift!

Picadillo de Turkey

Serves 6

222 calories
8g fat
14g carbohydrates
25g protein
132mg sodium
2g fiber

Ingredients

1½ pounds 90 percent lean
    ground turkey
1 clove fresh garlic, minced
½ teaspoon all-purpose
    seasoning
1 cup white onions, chopped
2 teaspoons cumin
1 cup tomatoes, diced
1 tablespoon tomato paste
¼ cup cilantro, chopped
¼ cup raisins
1 cup baking potatoes, cubed
1 cup water

Picadillo is a Cuban dish that is typically made with ground beef. It's often used for stuffed potatoes and tacos and is commonly served with mixed vegetables.

1. Spray large skillet with nonstick spray. Add turkey, olive oil, garlic, and all-purpose seasoning to skillet. Cook on medium high for 5 to 8 minutes, using a spatula to stir and chop turkey meat.

2. Add onions, tomatoes, tomato paste, cumin, and cilantro to skillet. Cook for 5 minutes on medium heat.

3. Add raisins, potatoes, and water. Simmer for another 8 to 10 minutes.

Turkey Sausage and Potato Bake

Sausages are spiced meats typically used for their powerful flavor. Substituting turkey sausage for your regular sausage is a healthy alternative that doesn't compromise flavor.

1. Coat a 9" × 13" baking dish with cooking spray.

2. In a bowl, mix all ingredients except for mozzarella. Mix well and pour into sprayed dish. Top with mozzarella and cover with foil.

3. Bake at 365°F for 30 to 35 minutes.

Skin Is In!

If you keep the skin on your potatoes instead of peeling them, you'll preserve tons of nutrients. The skin is packed with phytonutrient carotenoids and flavonoids. It is also a tremendous source of fiber. In the future, save some energy and don't peel those potatoes.

Serves 6

227 calories
5g fat
24g carbohydrates
22g protein
1,081mg sodium
3g fiber

Ingredients
4 cups baking potatoes, cubed
2 cups turkey kielbasa sausage, sliced
2 cups zucchini, sliced
1 cup yellow onions, chopped
½ cup chicken broth
½ teaspoon kosher salt
¼ teaspoon black pepper
2 teaspoons flour
1 clove fresh garlic, minced
1 cup shredded fat-free mozzarella cheese

Herbed Bread Stuffing with Mushrooms and Turkey Sausage

Serves 6

207 calories
5g fat
22g carbohydrates
17g protein
1,178mg sodium
2g fiber

Ingredients

1 clove fresh garlic, minced
½ teaspoon all-purpose
    seasoning
1 cup yellow onions, chopped
4 cups bread stuffing
½ cup carrots, chopped
½ cup celery, chopped
1 cup white mushrooms,
    sliced
2 cups turkey kielbasa
    sausage, sliced
1 cup chicken broth
1 tablespoon parsley
1 teaspoon sage
1 teaspoon thyme
¼ cup Egg Beaters

To prevent your eyes from watering, peel onions under running water. You can also find protective eyewear that's specifically made for chefs.

1. Mix all ingredients together well in a large bowl.

2. Coat a 9" × 13" baking dish with nonstick spray. Pour mixture into the dish and cover with foil.

3. Bake at 350°F for 25 minutes.

4. Remove foil and bake for another 5 minutes or until top is golden brown.

Chapter 12
Vegetarian

Veggie Sensation

Serves 6

126 calories
3g fat
22g carbohydrates
4g protein
635mg sodium
6g fiber

Ingredients
3 cups broccoli florets
2½ cups bell peppers, sliced
2 cups yellow onions, sliced
½ cup sun-dried tomatoes
1/3 cup roasted red peppers
1 teaspoon all-purpose seasoning
½ teaspoon dried basil
3 cups marinara sauce

Rinse raw fruits and vegetables under running water. Use a vegetable brush to help clean rough-skinned produce. Cut away rotten or bruised spots; bacteria thrive in them.

1. Cook all vegetables in a large nonstick skillet on medium heat. Season with all-purpose seasoning and basil.

2. When veggies are tender (onions browned), add marinara.

3. Continue to cook until sauce begins to bubble.

One Veggie Meal Per Week Challenge
Veggies are ridiculously low in fat and calories, and they're also super high in nutrition. Challenge yourself to eat at least one purely veggie meal per week. When you're good at that, try eating a purely vegetarian meal more often; your fab abs will come sooner!

Mixed-Beans Enchilada Verde

The enchilada sauce and cilantro in this recipe create quite an amazing flavor, but more importantly, the beans pack a ton of protein into this dish.

1. Mix first 9 ingredients and ¼ cup green enchilada sauce.

2. Coat a 9" × 13" baking dish with nonstick spray. Lay 4 tortillas in the dish. Cover with half of bean mixture.

3. Place 4 tortillas over bean mixture, followed by the remaining bean mixture.

4. Top with last 4 tortillas, ¼ cup enchilada sauce, and mozzarella cheese.

5. Cover with foil and bake at 400°F for 25 to 30 minutes.

Serves 8

419 calories
5g fat
76g carbohydrates
20g protein
674mg sodium
14g fiber

Ingredients

1 cup tomatoes, diced
2 cups white beans, cooked
2 cups pinto beans, cooked
2 cups black beans, cooked
½ teaspoon all-purpose seasoning
1 clove fresh garlic, minced
1 cup white onions, chopped
¼ cup cilantro, chopped
½ cup low-sodium chicken broth
½ cup green enchilada sauce, divided
12 whole wheat tortillas
¼ cup shredded fat-free mozzarella cheese

Quick Broccoli-Cauliflower Meal

This is a super simple recipe you can make in less than 10 minutes. Using the microwave is nothing to be ashamed of, especially if it makes it more convenient for you to eat healthy food.

1. Place veggies in a plastic bowl and microwave for 7 minutes.

2. Cover veggies with marinara and microwave for 90 seconds.

3. Sprinkle with Parmesan and enjoy.

Luis Black Bean Burrito

In order to fold tortillas into a perfect burrito, be sure to cover the tortillas with a damp paper towel and heat them in the microwave for 20 seconds.

1. Mix all ingredients except tortillas and cheese.

2. Coat a 9" × 13" baking dish with nonstick spray.

3. Divide mixture equally among 6 tortillas and fold each tortilla into a burrito.

4. Place each burrito in dish and top with Cheddar cheese.

5. Cover with foil and bake at 375°F for 20 minutes or until cheese melts.

Veggie Kabobs

These kabobs go well on top of Spaghetti Squash (page 135). Spaghetti squash is a fabulous low-calorie alternative to both pasta and rice.

1. Cut all the veggies into 2-inch chunks. Put the veggies on skewers and barbecue for 15 minutes, turning frequently. When grill marks appear to be steaming, veggies are done.

2. Cap ends of skewers with a pineapple chunk.

3. Brush veggies and fruit with teriyaki and serve.

Power to the Pepper!

Most people associate oranges with vitamin C. You may be surprised to know that one medium bell pepper contains 190 percent of your recommended daily intake of vitamin C, while 1 orange only provides 130 percent. Both are fabulously nutritious, but the power of the pepper should not be ignored.

Serves 4

128 calories
1g fat
29g carbohydrates
5g protein
570mg sodium
5g fiber

Ingredients
3 bell peppers (1 green, 1 red, and 1 yellow)
2 cups cherry tomatoes
2 medium zucchinis
1 small red onion
16 skewers
1 cup pineapple chunks
½ cup low-sodium teriyaki sauce

Spinach Lasagna Rolls

You can use fresh spinach in this recipe instead of frozen. Use 4 cups of fresh spinach if you plan to make this substitution. Frozen spinach is very dense, which is why this recipe only calls for 1 cup.

1. Mix garlic, all-purpose seasoning, Parmesan cheese, ½ cup mozzarella cheese, tomatoes, oregano, basil, nutmeg, and sugar. Set aside.

2. Mix ricotta and spinach. Set aside.

3. Coat a 9" × 13" baking dish with nonstick spray.

4. Cut each lasagna noodle in half lengthwise. Place 2 tablespoons of each mixture on one end of lasagna noodle. Roll noodle around mixtures and place in dish. Repeat for all noodles. Top with marinara sauce and remaining mozzarella cheese.

5. Cover with foil and bake at 375°F for 25 minutes.

Serves 6

382 calories
2g fat
71g carbohydrates
21g protein
235mg sodium
3g fiber

Ingredients
1 clove fresh garlic, minced
½ teaspoon all-purpose seasoning
½ cup reduced-fat Parmesan cheese
1 cup shredded fat-free mozzarella, divided
1½ cups fat-free ricotta cheese
1 cup frozen spinach, thawed and drained
1 cup tomatoes, diced
1 teaspoon dried oregano
1 teaspoon dried basil
¼ teaspoon nutmeg
1 tablespoon sugar or Splenda
6 mixed grain lasagna noodles, cooked
1 cup marinara sauce

Fitz's Mexican Power Potato

Boca Meatless Ground Burger can be replaced with lean ground turkey or beef, but meatless ground burgers are less expensive than meat and they cook up much more quickly.

1. Bake potato in oven at 400°F for 15 to 20 minutes or microwave for 10 to 14 minutes or until the skin is crispy and inside is soft.

2. Cut the potato in half. Scoop out 90 percent of white potato insides and discard them.

3. In a small bowl, combine ground meatless burger with taco seasoning.

4. Flatten out the remaining potato skin and scoop seasoned burger and peppers into it. Top with cheese.

5. Place potato back in your oven of choice. Microwave for 1 minute or bake in a conventional oven for 3 minutes.

6. Top with salsa.

Muscle Mix
This power potato provides the perfect amount of protein and fiber to serve as an entire meal! A lot of people swear off potatoes because of their dreaded carbs. That's unnecessary. Removing much of the potato pulp and filling it with healthy proteins or veggies makes the potato a superb ingredient.

Serves 1

233 calories
1g fat
43g carbohydrates
19g protein
620mg sodium
7g fiber

Ingredients
1 medium baking potato
1 bag Boca Meatless Ground Burger
½ teaspoon taco seasoning
2 tablespoons bell peppers, diced
1 tablespoon reduced-fat shredded Cheddar mix
2 tablespoons salsa

Mama's Ratatouille with Tofu

Ratatouille is French stew. It's a combination of garden vegetables and root vegetables that originated with French peasants.

Serves 6

162 calories
4g fat
26g carbohydrates
11g protein
548mg sodium
6g fiber

Ingredients

1 clove fresh garlic, minced
1 cup carrots, sliced
1 cup sweet potatoes, cubed
2 tablespoons dried basil
½ cup bell peppers, diced
1 cup tomatoes, diced
1 teaspoon all-purpose
    seasoning
1 teaspoon cumin
2 cups zucchini, sliced
2 cups squash, sliced
2 cups kale, chopped
2 cups tomato sauce
1 tablespoon thyme
½ teaspoon black pepper
1 16-ounce package firm
    tofu, cubed

1. Add all ingredients to a large saucepan. Cook over medium-high heat until it boils.

2. Simmer for 20 minutes or until sweet potatoes are tender.

Muscle Myths

It's a myth that women will earn bodybuilder physiques from lifting weights. That type of muscle requires an extraordinary amount of effort, and most women can't achieve it naturally. Instead of adding bulk, weight training will help a woman become slimmer, stronger, and curvier.

Yummy White Bean Enchilada Casserole

You can use either canned or dry beans in this recipe. When cooking dry beans, you should soak them for 1 hour in warm water and then cook them on medium-low heat for 90 minutes.

1. Mix first 12 ingredients and ½ cup of enchilada sauce.

2. Coat a 9" × 13" baking dish with nonstick spray. Lay 4 tortillas on the bottom of the dish. Cover with half of the bean mixture. Place 4 tortillas over bean mixture, followed by the remaining bean mixture. Top with the last 4 tortillas, ½ cup enchilada sauce, and low-fat Cheddar cheese.

3. Cover with foil and bake at 400°F for 25 to 30 minutes.

Choosing Cheese
Cheese consumption can be a double-edged sword. On one side, cheese is very high in calcium. On the other, it is often very high in fat and calories. Your best bet is to seek out reduced-fat cheeses and stick to small portions.

Serves 8

473 calories
8g fat
78g carbohydrates
25g protein
733mg sodium
12g fiber

Ingredients
6 cups canned white beans
2 tablespoons green onions, sliced
½ teaspoon all-purpose seasoning
1 clove fresh garlic, minced
2 tablespoons green chilies, finely chopped
½ cup fat-free sour cream
1 teaspoon cumin
1 tablespoon cilantro, chopped
½ cup shredded light Cheddar cheese
½ cup bell peppers, diced
¼ cup white onions, diced
½ cup strained tomatoes, diced
1 cup enchilada sauce for topping
12 whole wheat tortillas
½ cup shredded fat-free Cheddar cheese for topping

Vegetarian Paella

This recipe is a vegetarian version of a traditional Spanish dish. The original paella uses a combination of seafood and vegetables.

1. Mix all ingredients and set aside.

2. Coat a large skillet with nonstick spray. Add mixture to skillet and stir-fry mixture on medium-high heat for 8 minutes.

3. Decrease heat to medium and continue to stir-fry for 5 minutes or until all liquid has been absorbed.

Serves 6

260 calories
4g fat
51g carbohydrates
8g protein
340mg sodium
7g fiber

Ingredients

½ tablespoon olive oil
4 cups brown rice, cooked
1 clove fresh garlic, minced
½ teaspoon all-purpose
   seasoning
1 cup tomatoes, diced
½ cup bell peppers, diced
½ cup white onions, diced
3 cups frozen mixed
   vegetables
1 cup white mushrooms,
   sliced
1 tablespoon parsley
1 cup vegetable broth
½ teaspoon thyme
¼ teaspoon black pepper
1 Sazon packet

No-Meat Loaf

To make your own bread crumbs, cube day-old wheat bread and bake for 15 minutes. Finish by crumbling the bread cubes in a plastic bag.

1. In a food processor, finely chop mixed vegetables, mushrooms, and bell peppers.

2. Coat a 9" × 13" dish with nonstick spray.

3. Mix all ingredients except tomato paste. Spread mixture into the baking dish and press flat. Top mixture with tomato paste and cover with foil. Bake at 365°F for 30 minutes.

White Mushrooms

White mushrooms are one of the most common types of mushrooms used in North America. They are great served raw with a veggie tray or cooked as part of a dish. In fact, the flavor increases with cooking. If you slice them, plan to use them quickly. Once they are cut, white mushrooms quickly spoil by turning brown and soft.

Serves 6

100 calories
2g fat
16g carbohydrates
6g protein
193mg sodium
4g fiber

Ingredients
3 cups California-blend mixed vegetables
1 cup white mushrooms, roughly sliced
1 cup bell peppers, roughly chopped
1 cup frozen spinach
1½ cups brown rice, cooked
1 tablespoon dried basil
2 tablespoons reduced-fat grated Parmesan cheese
2 tablespoons cider vinegar
¼ cup egg whites
1½ cups bread crumbs
½ teaspoon all-purpose seasoning
1 clove fresh garlic, minced
½ tablespoon olive oil
2 tablespoons tomato paste

Karahi Tofu

Since this dish is low on vegetables, serve it with mashed cauliflower or over a Caesar salad. The tofu is extremely flavorful.

Serves 6

71 calories
3g fat
4g carbohydrates
6g protein
27mg sodium
1g fiber

Ingredients

1 clove fresh garlic, minced
½ cup yellow onions, finely
    chopped
1 16-ounce package firm
    tofu, cubed
2 tablespoons sherry wine
1 teaspoon coriander
2 tablespoons cilantro,
    chopped
½ teaspoon all-purpose
    seasoning
1 bay leaf
½ teaspoon mint, finely
    chopped

1. Coat a skillet with nonstick spray and heat over medium heat. Add garlic and onions to skillet. Sauté for 3 minutes. Add remaining ingredients to skillet.

2. Cook on medium-low heat for 12 to 15 minutes, stirring often.

Celebrity Slim-Down Secrets

The secret to celebrities being slim is this: their jobs often depend on it! Imagine what you would look like if you were threatened with losing your career over a few pounds. Of course, many celebrities can hire trainers and chefs, but they still need to use restraint when eating and work their butts off.

Broccoli and Three-Cheese Bake

To change this recipe up a bit, substitute broccoli with fresh or frozen cauliflower or baby carrots.

1. Coat a 9" × 13" dish with nonstick spray.

2. Mix rice, ¼ cup Parmesan cheese, all-purpose seasoning, Italian herbs, and Egg Beaters. Lay rice mixture in dish, pressing to the bottom.

3. Mix broccoli, onions, garlic, mozzarella, and Cheddar cheese. Pour broccoli mixture over rice.

4. Combine milk, flour, and all-purpose seasoning and pour over broccoli. Top with bread crumbs and remaining Parmesan.

5. Cover with foil and bake at 400°F for 25 to 30 minutes.

Serves 6

250 calories
3g fat
38g carbohydrates
18g protein
452mg sodium
5g fiber

Ingredients
3 cups brown rice
½ cup grated reduced fat Parmesan cheese, divided
½ teaspoon all-purpose seasoning
½ teaspoon Italian herbs
¼ cup Egg Beaters
4 cups frozen broccoli
1 cup white onions, chopped
1 clove fresh garlic, minced
½ cup shredded fat-free mozzarella cheese
½ cup shredded fat-free Cheddar cheese
½ cup skim milk
1 tablespoon flour
½ teaspoon all-purpose seasoning
¼ cup bread crumbs
¼ cup reduced-fat grated Parmesan cheese

Ginger and Orange Garden Veggies

When you cook snow peas in their pod, you preserve a truckload of fiber and the snow peas' natural flavor!

1. Mix ginger, sugar, all-purpose seasoning, garlic, soy sauce, olive oil, cornstarch, and orange juice in a large bowl. Add all vegetables and mix well to coat veggies.

2. Place vegetables in a steamer and cook for 8 to 12 minutes or until tender.

Serves 6

97 calories
3g fat
17g carbohydrates
4g protein
157mg sodium
5g fiber

Ingredients

1 teaspoon ground ginger
½ teaspoon sugar or Splenda
½ teaspoon all-purpose
  seasoning
1 clove fresh garlic, minced
½ cup orange slices
1 cup red onions, chopped
1 tablespoon low-sodium soy
  sauce
1 tablespoon olive oil
1 teaspoon cornstarch
½ cup freshly squeezed
  orange juice
3 cups broccoli chunks
2 cups cauliflower chunks
2 cups carrot chunks
2 cups snow peas in pod

Zulu Tofu in Spicy Red Sauce

Berbere is a delicious African spice made with a precise blend of red pepper, black pepper, ginger, cinnamon, and cloves. Try this spice in stews or tomato-based sauces.

1. Coat deep skillet with nonstick spray and heat over medium-high heat. Add broth, wine, and tomato paste to skillet. Mix well to dissolve paste.

2. Add remaining ingredients to skillet and cook for 15 minutes. Simmer for 5 to 8 minutes or until sauce thickens.

Round Is Risky

Men with waistline circumferences over 40 inches and women with waists greater than 35 inches have a significantly greater risk of a heart attack than their slimmer pals. Not only will utilizing the recipes in this book and exercising help you look better, it will help you live longer!

Serves 6

126 calories
4g fat
14g carbohydrates
8g protein
355mg sodium
2g fiber

Ingredients

1 cup vegetable broth
½ cup red wine
2 tablespoons tomato paste
1 16-ounce package firm tofu, cubed
2 tablespoons freshly squeezed lemon juice
6 lemon slices
2 tablespoons cilantro, chopped
½ teaspoon all-purpose seasoning
1 clove fresh garlic, minced
1 tablespoon dry ginger
1 cup white onion, chopped
½ teaspoon nutmeg
½ teaspoon dried cardamon
2 teaspoons Berbere African Spice (page 162)

Tofu and Broccoli Casserole

Evaporated milk substitutes for fresh milk well because it has a longer shelf life. To return this dehydrated milk back to its original state, add equal parts of water to it.

1. Coat a 9" × 13" baking dish with nonstick spray.

2. Mix all ingredients except bread crumbs and Parmesan in a large bowl. Pour mixture into dish. Top with bread crumbs and Parmesan cheese.

3. Cover with foil and bake at 370°F for 30 to 40 minutes. Uncover and bake for another 10 minutes or until golden brown.

Serves 6

228 calories
4g fat
31g carbohydrates
18g protein
540mg sodium
2g fiber

Ingredients
½ cup white onions, chopped
3 cups broccoli florets
½ teaspoon all-purpose
    seasoning
1 clove fresh garlic, minced
1 cup fat-free evaporated
    milk
1 16-ounce package firm
    tofu, cubed
½ cup fat-free mayonnaise
1 cup low-sodium mushroom
    soup
¼ cup flour
1 teaspoon Worcestershire
    sauce
Dash of nutmeg
¼ cup wine
½ cup fat-free grated
    Parmesan cheese
½ teaspoon black pepper
¼ cup bread crumbs
½ cup fat-free grated
    Parmesan cheese

Cheesy Vegetable Penne Florentine

This dish can be assembled ahead of time and stored overnight in the refrigerator. Add an additional 10 minutes of cooking time to original recipe instructions.

1. Coat 9" × 13" baking dish with nonstick spray. In a large mixing bowl, combine all ingredients except ¼ cup Cheddar and ¼ cup Parmesan. Add mixture to the dish. Top with ¼ cup Cheddar and ¼ cup Parmesan.

2. Cover with foil and bake at 360°F for 25 to 30 minutes.

3. Uncover and bake for additional 5 to 10 minutes or until cheese is melted.

Choose Your Carbs Wisely

Carbohydrates are not evil! In fact, they're the primary sources of fuel for our bodies and brains. White bread, pasta, and rice will provide you with a quick spike in energy, but you'll quickly crash. Ouch! Carbohydrates from fruits, vegetables, and whole grains offer long-lasting energy with no crashes at all.

Serves 6

183 calories
4g fat
22g carbohydrates
17g protein
546mg sodium
5g fiber

Ingredients

1 clove fresh garlic, minced
½ teaspoon all-purpose seasoning
3 cups fresh spinach
1 cup white mushrooms, sliced
½ cup bell peppers, diced
1 teaspoon oregano
1 cup fat-free cottage cheese
2 cups whole wheat penne pasta, cooked
3 cups frozen California-blend veggies
½ cup shredded fat-free Cheddar cheese
¼ cup skim milk
1 cup cream of chicken soup
¼ cup shredded low-fat Cheddar cheese
¼ cup reduced-fat grated Parmesan cheese

Greek Tofu

Serves 6

82 calories
4g fat
8g carbohydrates
7g protein
30mg sodium
2g fiber

Ingredients

1 clove fresh garlic, minced
1 cup red onions, chopped
1 cup bell peppers, diced
4 tablespoons freshly
   squeezed lemon juice
1 cup tomatoes, diced
½ teaspoon all-purpose
   seasoning
1 teaspoon dried basil
1 teaspoon oregano
1 16-ounce package firm
   tofu, cubed

This dish includes red onions instead of white or yellow because they add a sweeter flavor that tames the acidity of the lemon juice and tomatoes.

1. Mix all ingredients in a large bowl. Pour ingredients into a large skillet coated with nonstick spray.

2. Cook on medium high for 15 minutes, stirring often. Cover and simmer for 10 minutes, stirring often.

The Power of Protein

Protein is your body's power source. It's the nutrient your body relies on to make muscles, hair, fingernails, skin, and more. You need to consume protein each and every day to help your body create and recreate new cells. Did you know that some of your cells need to be rebuilt every three days?

Fiery Black Bean-Poblano Casserole

Poblano chilies are mild chili peppers, and they are one of the most commonly used chili peppers in Mexico. They can be stuffed, baked, or used in mole sauce.

1. In a large mixing bowl, combine all ingredients except for tortillas, skim milk, flour, and Cheddar cheese.

2. Spray 9" × 13" baking dish with nonstick spray. Cover bottom of baking dish with 4 tortillas. Spread half of mixture over tortillas. Top with 4 more tortillas and remaining mixture. Top with remaining tortillas.

3. Combine skim milk and flour; mix well. Pour white sauce over tortillas and top with Cheddar.

4. Cover with foil and bake at 360°F for 30 to 35 minutes.

Royal Beans

Beans are so jam-packed with nutrients that they qualify as both a vegetable and a protein. That's kind of like being both king and queen of the prom! They're even stuffed with fiber and the good kinds of carbohydrates.

Serves 8

319 calories
4g fat
67g carbohydrates
24g protein
793mg sodium
10g fiber

Ingredients

1 clove fresh garlic, minced
½ teaspoon all-purpose
    seasoning
½ cup bell peppers, diced
2 cups frozen corn
1 cup nonfat shredded
    Mexican cheese blend
¼ cup cilantro, chopped
2 teaspoons poblano chilies,
    finely chopped
¼ cup Egg Beaters
1 cup fat-free cottage cheese
3 cups black beans, cooked
    and drained
½ cup green onions, sliced
12 whole wheat tortillas
½ cup skim milk
2 tablespoons flour
¼ cup shredded nonfat
    Cheddar cheese

Green Chili and Herb Vegetables

Consuming lots of veggies, fruits, folic acid, selenium-rich foods, and fiber and avoiding trans fats and saturated fats will lower your risk for cancer.

Serves 6

169 calories
2g fat
36g carbohydrates
5g protein
464mg sodium
6g fiber

Ingredients

2 teaspoons chili powder
½ teaspoon all-purpose
*   seasoning*
1 teaspoon cumin
1 teaspoon paprika
¼ teaspoon ground red
*   pepper*
1 clove fresh garlic, minced
2 cups broccoli florets
2 cups carrots, sliced
2 cups sweet potatoes, diced
2 cups frozen corn
2 teaspoons green chilis,
*   finely chopped*
2 tablespoons freshly
*   squeezed lemon juice*
2 teaspoons oregano
1½ cups vegetable broth

1. Coat a large skillet with nonstick spray. Combine all ingredients in a large mixing bowl. Add vegetable mixture to skillet.

2. Cook on medium-high heat for 15 minutes, stirring often. Cover and simmer for 10 to 15 minutes or until sweet potatoes are tender.

Brawny Broccoli

Broccoli contains sulforaphane, a powerful cancer-fighting compound. Eat some on a regular basis and you may reduce your risk of getting lung, bladder, and breast cancer. You can also find this powerful phytochemical in other cruciferous vegetables such as cauliflower, cabbage, and kale.

Vegetable Lasagna

This veggie lasagna would be great served with a starter-size Caesar salad. Don't forget to always choose fat-free dressings and serve them on the side.

1. Mix first 9 ingredients and set aside.

2. Coat a 9" × 13" baking dish with nonstick spray. Spread ½ cup marinara sauce over bottom of dish. Layer ⅓ of the lasagna noodles over marinara. Cover with half of the veggie mixture. Cover with another ⅓ of the lasagna noodles and top with remaining veggie mixture.

3. Top with remaining ⅓ of lasagna noodles, ½ cup marinara, and mozzarella cheese.

4. Cover with foil and bake in oven at 375°F for 35 minutes.

Circuit Workout #2
Here's a quick circuit workout to do while you're waiting for that lasagna to bake. Do 20 squats and 20 pushups. Do 3 sets of planks, holding for 30 seconds each time. Do 30 lunges and 15 dips. Repeat as many times as you can before the oven timer dings!

Serves 10

343 calories
3g fat
53g carbohydrates
25g protein
588mg sodium
5g fiber

Ingredients

1 10-ounce bag spinach
4 cups California-blend vegetable medley
2 cups fat-free cottage cheese
¼ cup grated reduced-fat Parmesan cheese
1 clove fresh garlic, minced
½ teaspoon all-purpose seasoning
½ cup Egg Beaters
1 cup white mushrooms, sliced
½ cup yellow onions, chopped
1 cup marinara sauce
1 box whole wheat lasagna noodles, cooked
1 cup shredded fat-free mozzarella

Tofu and Asparagus Stir-Fry

You might know that asparagus provides tons of folic acid, potassium, and fiber, but were you aware that the early Egyptians and Romans used it as a natural diuretic?

Serves 6

148 calories
8g fat
13g carbohydrates
9g protein
426mg sodium
3g fiber

Ingredients
½ tablespoon peanut oil
1 teaspoon sesame oil
1 cup vegetable broth
2 cups fresh asparagus, cut in
    2-inch segments
1 16-ounce package firm
    tofu, cubed
1 clove fresh garlic, minced
½ teaspoon all-purpose
    seasoning
1 cup green onions, sliced
1 tablespoon ground ginger
1 tablespoon low-sodium soy
    sauce
1 tablespoon Worcestershire
1 teaspoon Splenda brown
    sugar
1 teaspoon cornstarch
2 tablespoons sesame seeds

1. Coat a large skillet with nonstick spray and heat over medium heat. Add peanut oil, sesame oil, vegetable broth, and asparagus. Cook for 8 to 10 minutes.

2. Add remaining ingredients to skillet. Stirring often, cook for 15 to 20 minutes or until asparagus are tender and sauce thickens.

Tofu and Vegetables with Feta Sauce

This feta sauce is a much lower-fat version than the original. Combine the last 4 ingredients in this recipe to make your own and use it for other dishes.

1. Mix all ingredients. Coat a large skillet with nonstick spray. Add mixture to skillet.

2. Cook on medium high for 15 minutes, stirring often. Cover and simmer for 15 minutes or until sauce thickens, stirring often.

Protein from Vegetables

Vegetarians do not eat meat, the most obvious source of protein, but there are plenty of plants that can provide more than enough of this powerful nutrient. Soybeans (used to make tofu), beans, nuts, peanut butter, sunflower seeds, and pumpkin seeds are awesome choices. Protein is a vital component of a healthy body, so be sure to include it in your diet.

Serves 6

121 calories
3g fat
10g carbohydrates
13g protein
381mg sodium
2g fiber

Ingredients

1 16-ounce package firm
   tofu, cubed
2 tablespoons balsamic
   vinegar
1 clove fresh garlic, minced
½ teaspoon all-purpose
   seasoning
1 teaspoon oregano
½ teaspoon thyme
3 cups frozen California-
   blend veggies
1 cup skim milk
½ cup fat-free feta cheese
1 teaspoon lemon juice
1 tablespoon flour

Tofu with Black Bean Sauce

This dish would go very well with an asparagus salad or any variety of stir-fried vegetables.

Serves 6

76 calories
3g fat
18g carbohydrates
7g protein
127mg sodium
1g fiber

Ingredients

1 clove fresh garlic, minced
½ teaspoon all-purpose seasoning
1 cup orange juice
1 tablespoon black bean paste
1 tablespoon low-sodium soy sauce
1½ teaspoons sugar or Splenda
1½ teaspoons cornstarch
¼ teaspoon black pepper
1 16-ounce package firm tofu, cut in large slices

1. Combine all ingredients except tofu. Coat large skillet with nonstick spray. Place tofu slices on skillet and cover with mixture.

2. Cook on medium heat for 15 to 18 minutes, turning once.

Holidays, Not Holimonths

To avoid the need to drop ten for the New Year, take a look at the season. The winter holidays are about spending time with friends and family and giving thanks. They're not about gluttony! Enjoy a small indulgence on your specific holiday dates and stick to your standard fitness habits during the other days in December.

Eggplant Enchilada Casserole

Enchiladas are a kind of Mexican lasagna that use corn tortillas for layering instead of pasta. For a healthier version, use whole wheat tortillas instead of corn tortillas.

1. Mix the first 10 ingredients together and set aside.

2. Coat a 9" × 13" baking dish with nonstick spray. Pour ¼ cup enchilada sauce on the bottom of the dish. Place 4 tortillas in the dish and add half of the eggplant mixture. Layer with 4 more tortillas and top with remaining eggplant mixture.

3. Add remaining 4 tortillas and top with remaining enchilada sauce and cheese.

4. Cover with foil and bake at 375°F for 35 to 40 minutes.

Usher Muscles

You know those vertical muscles that run right inside the hips, made famous by hip-hop artist Usher? They're called hip flexors. In order to develop yours, do exercises in which you lift your entire leg straight up in front of you. Front kicks, pikes, and mountain climbers are ideal exercises for these muscles.

Serves 8

294 calories
8g fat
46g carbohydrates
11g protein
759mg sodium
5g fiber

Ingredients

*4 cups eggplant, cubed
½ cup red onions, chopped
½ teaspoon all-purpose
   seasoning
1 clove fresh garlic, minced
½ teaspoon oregano
½ cup enchilada sauce
½ cup shredded low-fat
   Cheddar cheese
1 cup tomatoes, diced
½ teaspoon cumin
¼ cup vegetable broth
½ cup enchilada sauce
12 whole wheat tortillas
½ cup shredded low-fat
   Cheddar cheese*

Chapter 13
Beef and Pork

Spicy and Sour Pork with Cabbage

You can use prepackaged sliced cabbage to reduce preparation time on this recipe. For the Chinese chili sauce, you can use the Thai hot chili sauce sriracha (look for the Huy Fong brand).

1. Coat a skillet with nonstick spray. Add pork, garlic, and all-purpose seasoning to skillet. Sauté on medium-high heat for 8 minutes, stirring often.

2. Mix remaining ingredients and add to skillet. Simmer for 8 to 10 minutes. Add water if mixture gets too dry.

Acapulco Steak Chunks

Baking black beans from scratch takes quite a long time. If you are in a hurry, buy the canned variety. They're still very nutritious and much faster when every second counts.

Serves 6

240 calories
6g fat
17g carbohydrates
29g protein
577mg sodium
4g fiber

Ingredients
*1½ pounds top round sirloin
  chunks
1 clove fresh garlic, minced
½ teaspoon all-purpose
  seasoning
1 cup frozen corn
½ cup cilantro, chopped
½ cup beef broth
½ cup celery, sliced
1 cup white onions, sliced
2 cups salsa
1½ cups black beans, canned
1 teaspoon oregano
¼ teaspoon black pepper*

1. Coat a skillet with nonstick spray. Add sirloin, garlic, and all-purpose seasoning to skillet. Sauté on medium high for 8 minutes, stirring often.

2. Mix remaining ingredients and add to skillet. Simmer for 8 to 10 minutes. Add water if mixture gets too dry.

Weight Fluctuations
It's frustrating to see your weight increase 5 pounds in one day. Fortunately, that weight gain is probably not real. In order to gain just 1 pound of fat, you must consume 3,600 calories. Ask yourself if you ate enough to account for the weight gain. If not, it's probably just bloating or water retention.

Beef and Sugar Snap Peas

Cornstarch is an excellent thickener, and it's used in this recipe to keep the sauce from getting too runny.

1. Coat a skillet with nonstick spray. Add beef, garlic, and all-purpose seasoning to skillet. Sauté on medium high for 8 minutes, stirring often.

2. Mix remaining ingredients and add to skillet. Simmer for 8 to 10 minutes.

Shoe Shopping

Before you begin any sort of exercise program, make sure you have the proper footwear. Shoes protect your feet and legs like a helmet protects a football player. Runners need lots of support at the forefoot and heel to reduce impact, while dancers need a smooth-soled shoe for pivoting. Protect your feet and they'll keep you moving in the right direction!

Serves 6

349 calories
9g fat
33g carbohydrates
31g protein
1,177mg sodium
5g fiber

Ingredients

1½ pounds round sirloin chunks
1 clove fresh garlic, minced
½ teaspoon all-purpose seasoning
3 tablespoons low-sodium soy sauce
1 cup chicken broth
½ cup hoisin sauce
1½ cups white onions, chunks
1 tablespoon cornstarch
1 tablespoon sesame oil
1½ tablespoons ground ginger
3 cups sugar snap peas, fresh or frozen
1½ cups carrots, sliced

Creamy Curried Beef and Onions

When cooking beef, make sure you stick with the leaner cuts. Top sirloin, eye of round, and bottom round cuts have less than 3 grams of saturated fats per serving.

1. Coat a skillet with nonstick spray. Add beef, garlic, and all-purpose seasoning to skillet. Sauté on medium high for 8 minutes, stirring often.

2. Mix remaining ingredients except sour cream and add to skillet. Simmer for 8 to 10 minutes. Add sour cream and mix well. Simmer for another 5 minutes.

Curry Powder
Curry powder is not a standard flavor like ginger. There are many varieties, but the most common spices used to create it are coriander, cumin, turmeric, and fenugreek. Ginger, nutmeg, black pepper, and garlic are also commonly used.

Serves 6

146 calories
3g fat
12g carbohydrates
18g protein
302mg sodium
2g fiber

Ingredients
1½ pounds round sirloin chunks
1 clove fresh garlic, minced
½ teaspoon all-purpose seasoning
½ teaspoon black pepper
1 teaspoon ground ginger
1 teaspoon jalapeño peppers, finely chopped
2 cups yellow onions, sliced
2 cups tomatoes, diced
1 tablespoon curry powder
1 teaspoon coriander
1 cup beef broth
1 cup fat-free sour cream

Chili-Beef with Corn and Mixed Peppers

Beef-eaters beware! Did you know a 10-ounce prime rib packs about 1,000 calories and between 35 to 40 grams of saturated fat? For flat abs and a healthy heart, avoid prime rib altogether or stick with very small portions of it.

1. Coat a skillet with nonstick spray. Add beef, garlic, and all-purpose seasoning to skillet. Sauté on medium-high heat for 8 minutes, stirring often.

2. Mix remaining ingredients and add to skillet. Simmer for 8 to 10 minutes.

Serves 6

231 calories
6g fat
16g carbohydrates
29g protein
302mg sodium
2g fiber

Ingredients

1½ pounds top sirloin
1 clove fresh garlic, minced
½ teaspoon all-purpose
    seasoning
2 cups frozen corn
½ cup bell peppers, diced
½ cup white onions, diced
¼ cup cilantro, chopped
1 tablespoon lemon juice
2 teaspoons brown sugar
½ teaspoon onion powder
1 teaspoon oregano
½ teaspoon paprika
½ teaspoon red pepper
½ teaspoon cumin
¼ teaspoon black pepper
1 cup beef broth

Garlic and Herb Meatloaf

The FDA recommends you not eat ground beef that is pink. Cook ground beef to at least 160°F (71°C). Make sure your food thermometer is clean before you use it!

1. In a large bowl, mix all ingredients except tomato paste and Worcestershire sauce.

2. Coat a 9" × 13" baking dish with nonstick spray. Add beef mixture to dish and mold into a log shape.

3. In a smaller bowl, mix tomato paste and Worcestershire sauce and top meatloaf with it.

4. Cover with foil and bake at 350°F for 35 minutes. Uncover and bake for an additional 5 to 10 minutes.

Abtastic!
Thank goodness this recipe takes a while to bake! You've got plenty of time to jump on your treadmill or stepper at home and work out. Throw on a pair of sneakers and set your machine to stop in 25 minutes; this will give you plenty of time to check on the progress of your meatloaf.

Serves 6

383 calories
4g fat
19g carbohydrates
15g protein
272mg sodium
3g fiber

Ingredients
1½ pounds 90 percent lean ground beef
½ cup ketchup
½ teaspoon all-purpose seasoning
1 clove fresh garlic, minced
½ cup Egg Beaters
2 tablespoons parsley
1 tablespoon dried basil
½ cup white onions, chopped
½ teaspoon black pepper
1 cup oats
½ cup tomatoes, diced
2 tablespoons tomato paste for dressing
1 tablespoon Worcestershire sauce for dressing

Pork and Stir-Fry Veggies with Spicy Asian Sauce

Ingredients

1½ pounds pork tenderloin
    chunks
1 clove fresh garlic, minced
½ teaspoon all-purpose
    seasoning
¼ cup hoisin sauce
¼ cup low-sodium ketchup
2 teaspoons low-sodium soy
    sauce
¼ teaspoon red pepper flakes
1 teaspoon sesame oil
1 cup bell peppers, sliced
1 cup zucchini, sliced
1 teaspoon ground ginger
½ cup green onions, sliced
1 teaspoon sesame seeds

Slice the vegetables up to a day in advance to save yourself some time during the cooking process.

1. Coat a skillet with nonstick spray. Add pork, garlic, and all-purpose seasoning to skillet. Sauté on medium high for 8 minutes, stirring often.

2. Mix remaining ingredients and add to skillet. Simmer for 8 to 10 minutes. Add water if mixture gets too dry.

Healthy Here, Healthy There
Vacations are designed for people to get away from the daily grind, see something new, and have some fun. They are not designed for people to blow their healthy habits and gain ten pounds as quickly as possible. Always include exercise as part of your day wherever you are and stick with healthy eating habits.

Exclusive Pork Stroganoff

Stroganoff is a Russian dish. In this recipe, lower the heat before adding the sour cream for a creamier sauce.

1. Coat a skillet with nonstick spray. Add pork, flour, garlic, and all-purpose seasoning to skillet. Sauté on medium high for 8 minutes, stirring often.

2. Mix remaining ingredients except sour cream and add to skillet. Simmer for 8 to 10 minutes. Add sour cream and simmer for 5 minutes, stirring often.

The Term "Edible" Is Subjective

Just because they make it doesn't mean you have to eat it! There are thousands of foods lining grocery stores, but not all of them are worthy of that fabulous body of yours. Are crackers and cookies tasty? Yes! Are they good for you? No! Choose foods by their ability to bring you closer to or farther from your point B.

Serves 6

177 calories
4g fat
8g carbohydrates
26g protein
157mg sodium
1g fiber

Ingredients

1½ pounds pork tenderloin, cut in chunks
2 tablespoons flour
1 clove fresh garlic, minced
½ teaspoon all-purpose seasoning
3 tablespoons tomato paste
2 cups chicken broth
1 cup white mushrooms, sliced
½ cup bell peppers, diced
1 teaspoon nutmeg
¼ teaspoon black pepper
½ cup fat-free sour cream

Orange Pork with Onions

To add variety to this recipe, stir in some cashews at the end of the cooking process and serve over Spaghetti Squash (page 135).

<table>
<tr><td>

Serves 6

195 calories
4g fat
12g carbohydrates
26g protein
524mg sodium
2g fiber

Ingredients

1½ pounds pork tenderloin, chunks
2 tablespoons cornstarch
1 clove fresh garlic, minced
½ teaspoon all-purpose seasoning
1 cup chicken broth
½ cup orange juice
3 tablespoons low-sodium soy sauce
1 teaspoon chili powder
2 cups carrots, sliced
1 teaspoon ground ginger
1 cup yellow onions, sliced
½ teaspoon black pepper

</td></tr>
</table>

1. Coat a skillet with nonstick spray. Add pork, cornstarch, garlic, and all-purpose seasoning. Sauté on medium-high heat for 8 minutes, stirring often.

2. Mix remaining ingredients and add to skillet. Simmer for 8 to 10 minutes. Add water if mixture gets too dry.

Opposing Muscle Groups

It is vital to work opposing muscle groups when strength training. Opposing muscle groups are muscles that counterbalance each other. If you spend time training your abdominals, it's equally important to spend time training your erector spinae (the lower back). Superman exercises are a great choice for this. To do a Superman, lie face down on the floor and raise both straight arms and legs in to the air as if you are flying.

Honey and Dill Pork

Honey is a natural sweetener. When added to meat dishes, it creates a caramelizing effect that seals the juices and flavors of the meat as it cooks.

1. Coat a large skillet with nonstick spray. Mix all ingredients except pork and onions.

2. Dip pork in mixture and place in skillet on medium heat for 4 minutes on each side. Add onions and simmer for 3 to 5 minutes.

Serves 6

167 calories
4g fat
8g carbohydrates
24g protein
79mg sodium
0g fiber

Ingredients

1 clove fresh garlic, minced
½ teaspoon all-purpose seasoning
2 tablespoons honey
1 tablespoon dill (herb)
6 pork tenderloins, about ½-inch thick
1 cup white onions, sliced

Autumn Apple Chops

Apple cider could be substituted in this dish for the apple juice, and the chops would be delicious served over mashed cauliflower.

1. Coat a 9" × 13" baking dish with cooking spray. Evenly place pork chops on dish without crowding. Top pork with apple and onion slices.

2. Mix apple juice, garlic, all-purpose seasoning, and flour. Add juice mixture to pork dish.

3. Cover and bake at 350°F for 20 to 30 minutes or until internal temperature reaches 160°F.

Serves 6

186 calories
4g fat
12g carbohydrates
24g protein
80mg sodium
1g fiber

Ingredients

6 pork tenderloin chops, about ½-inch thick
1 cup Granny Smith apple slices
1 cup sliced white onions
1½ cups apple juice
1 teaspoon finely chopped fresh garlic
½ teaspoon all-purpose seasoning
1 tablespoon flour

Cuban Picadillo

Serves 6

382 calories
3g fat
19g carbohydrates
12g protein
144mg sodium
2g fiber

Ingredients

1½ pounds 90 percent lean
    ground beef
1 clove fresh garlic, minced
½ teaspoon all-purpose
    seasoning
½ cup yellow onions,
    chopped
½ cup bell peppers, diced
1 cup tomatoes, diced
1 tablespoon tomato paste
½ cup cooking wine
¼ cup green olives, sliced
1 teaspoon oregano
¼ teaspoon black pepper
1 teaspoon cumin
½ cup raisins
1 cup baking potatoes, cubed
½ cup water

When buying ground beef, make sure you choose a package that is at least 90 percent lean. Seventy-five percent lean ground beef still packs 8 grams of saturated fat per 3 ounces—too much!

1. Coat a large skillet with nonstick spray. Add beef, garlic, and all-pur-pose seasoning to skillet. Cook on medium high for 5 to 8 minutes, using a spatula to stir and chop beef.

2. Add onions, bell peppers, tomatoes, tomato paste, wine, green olives, oregano, black pepper, and cumin to skillet. Cook for 5 minutes.

3. Add raisins, potatoes, and water. Simmer for another 8 to 15 minutes or until potatoes are fork tender.

Lean Pork Chops with Ginger-Cherry Sauce

Did you know that cherries are full of anthocyanins? Studies show that this makes them great for reducing inflammation after a too-tough workout.

1. Coat a 9" × 13" baking dish with nonstick spray. Lay pork tenderloins in the dish, being careful not to crowd them. Mix remaining ingredients and pour over chops.

2. Cover with foil and bake at 350°F for 25 to 35 minutes or until internal temperature of the pork reaches 160°F.

Bananas about Cherries

Did you know that sweet cherries are full of potassium? One medium banana provides 13 percent of the recommended daily intake of potassium, while one cup of cherries provides 10 percent. Consume both on a regular basis and muscle cramps from your hard workouts will be fewer and farther between.

Serves 6

202 calories
6g fat
13g carbohydrates
24g protein
181mg sodium
0g fiber

Ingredients

6 pork tenderloin chops
2 teaspoons sesame oil
1 teaspoon all-purpose seasoning
½ teaspoon fresh garlic, minced
1 tablespoon low-sodium soy sauce
1 cup low-sugar cherry filling
2 teaspoons ground ginger
2 teaspoons rice vinegar

Citrus Crunch Pork Chops

Serves 6

208 calories
5g fat
17g carbohydrates
26g protein
155mg sodium
2g fiber

Ingredients

1½ cups bread crumbs
1 teaspoon finely chopped
    fresh garlic
½ teaspoon all-purpose
    seasoning
½ teaspoon paprika
6 pork tenderloin chops,
    about ½-inch thick
3 sliced oranges
2 sliced lemons

*This dish would be complete if served with a spinach and orange salad and a
side serving of a yogurt dressing or balsamic vinaigrette.*

1. Coat a 9" × 13" baking dish with cooking spray.

2. Mix bread crumbs, finely chopped fresh garlic, all-purpose seasoning,
   and paprika. Add pork chops to the mixture and coat well.

3. Place pork chops in dish and top with orange and lemon slices. Bake
   in oven at 350°F for 25 to 30 minutes.

Music Matters
*With a banging beat, sometimes it is just impossible not to start moving
your body. Music is a valuable and powerful fitness tool that should not
be ignored. Invest in an MP3 player or a boombox and let the music
move you.*

Yankee Pot Roast

A British study published in Pharmacology, Biochemistry and Behavior found that young adults significantly improved their word recall if they were given sage oil extract on a regular basis.

1. Add all ingredients to a large saucepan and cook on medium high for 8 to 10 minutes.

2. Reduce heat and simmer for 20 to 25 minutes. Add water if gravy dries out.

Circuit Workout #3
You've got 25 minutes, so spend it exercising! Jump rope for 5 minutes. Do 5 sets of pikes (page 12), holding each as long as you can. Do 40 lunges. Grab a pair of challenging weights and do bicep curls. Repeat this circuit as many times as you can before your food is ready.

Serves 6

339 calories
5g fat
43g carbohydrates
29g protein
537mg sodium
4g fiber

Ingredients

1½ pounds top sirloin, in chunks
1 teaspoon finely chopped fresh garlic
½ teaspoon all-purpose seasoning
2 cups yucca, in chunks
2 cups sliced carrots
2 cups baking potatoes, in big chunks
2 cups beef broth
1 cup yellow onions, in chunks
1 teaspoon thyme
½ teaspoon sage
3 bay leaves
½ teaspoon black pepper

Pork and Chili Verde

When cooking pork, it is important to remember not to overcook it since it quickly becomes tough. It should always be cooked to an internal temperature of 160°F.

Serves 6

230 calories
5g fat
18g carbohydrates
26g protein
668mg sodium
2g fiber

Ingredients

1½ pounds pork tenderloin
    in chunks
1 teaspoon olive oil
2 teaspoons cornstarch
1 teaspoon finely chopped
    fresh garlic
½ teaspoon all-purpose
    seasoning
½ cup cilantro
1 teaspoon oregano
1 teaspoon cumin
2 cups tomatillo sauce
½ cup green chili sauce
¼ cup flour
½ teaspoon black pepper
3 cups water
3 cups yellow onions,
    chopped

1. Coat a skillet with nonstick spray. Add pork, olive oil, cornstarch, garlic, and all-purpose seasoning to skillet. Sauté on medium high for 8 minutes, stirring often.

2. Mix remaining ingredients and add to skillet. Simmer for 8 to 10 minutes or until internal temperature reaches 160°F. Add water if mixture gets too dry.

Home Sweet Home
Beyond working hard to achieve aesthetic beauty like flat abs, take care of your body so it will provide you with a life worth living. Your body is truly your home, and moving out is not an option! And if you take great care of your insides, your outsides will certainly look the way you want them too!

Stuffed Pork Loin with Onion Cranberry Sauce

Garnish this dish with flat-leaf parsley to make the red cranberry sauce pop.

1. Butterfly pork loin.

2. Combine apples, feta cheese, all-purpose seasoning, dried cranberries, garlic, onions, and cranberry sauce. Mix well.

3. Open pork loin and stuff with mixture. Tie with twine.

4. Spray a 9" × 13" baking dish with nonstick spray and place stuffed pork in it.

5. In separate bowl, mix cranberry juice, water, and Splenda. Pour over pork and cover with foil.

6. Bake at 375°F for 30 to 40 minutes or until thoroughly cooked and internal temperature reaches 160°F.

Serves 6

298 calories
7g fat
34g carbohydrates
26g protein
232mg sodium
2g fiber

Ingredients

1½ pounds boneless pork loin
1 cup chopped apples
¼ cup feta cheese
½ teaspoon all-purpose seasoning
2 tablespoons dried cranberries
1 teaspoon finely chopped fresh garlic
1 cup white onions, chopped
1 cup cranberry sauce
2' of twine, cut into 3 equal strips
1½ cups 100 percent cranberry juice
½ cup water
2 tablespoons Splenda

Mighty Meatloaf

Serves 6

333 calories
3g fat
7g carbohydrates
14g protein
227mg sodium
1g fiber

Ingredients
1½ pounds 90 percent lean
    ground beef
1 teaspoon finely chopped
    fresh garlic
½ teaspoon all-purpose
    seasoning
¼ cup bread crumbs
2 tablespoons ketchup
½ cup onions, chopped
1 tablespoon parsley
1 tablespoon mustard
1 teaspoon dried basil
¾ cup Egg Beaters
½ cup diced tomatoes

This dish is a great alternative to the meatloaf you probably had growing up. To make it even healthier, try using ground turkey instead of ground beef.

1. Coat a baking dish with cooking spray.

2. Mix all ingredients together. Shape into a dome, place on the baking dish, and cover with foil.

3. Bake at 350°F for 30 to 35 minutes.

Bouncing Around
To maximize both the healthiness and happiness of family reunions, holiday festivities, or birthday parties, rent a bounce house. It's the perfect activity to keep both adults and children moving, burning calories, and having fun! Another benefit: spending time in the bounce house will keep you away from the snacks all day.

Beef Chunks with Tropical Salsa

If you'd like to make your tropical fruit mix fresh and from scratch, dice and combine pineapples, cherries, peaches, and pears.

1. Coat a skillet with nonstick spray. Add sirloin, garlic, and all-purpose seasoning to skillet. Cook on medium-high heat for 4 minutes, stirring often.

2. Add remaining ingredients to pan. Cook on medium heat for 6 to 8 minutes, stirring often.

When Gaining Weight Is Great!
If you've been strength training with weights for a while and the exercises are becoming less than challenging, it's time to increase your weight! If you are not struggling to lift your weights by the time you get to 10 repetitions, they've become too light and you need to advance. Your body will only respond when it's challenged.

Serves 6

140 calories
4g fat
13g carbohydrates
14g protein
59mg sodium
1g fiber

Ingredients
*1½ pounds sirloin chunks
1 clove fresh garlic, minced
½ teaspoon all-purpose seasoning
4 teaspoons sesame seeds
1½ cups tropical fruit mix (without syrup)
2 tablespoons orange juice
½ cup bell peppers, sliced
½ cup yellow onions, sliced
2 tablespoons cilantro, chopped
1 teaspoon crushed red pepper*

Teppanyaki Beef Stir-Fry

This dish should be served immediately after it is cooked to prevent the beef from toughening up. Serve it with cellophane noodles.

1. Spray a nonstick skillet with cooking spray. Add beef and garlic to skillet. Cook on medium-high heat for 5 minutes, stirring often.

2. Add remaining ingredients to skillet. Lower heat to medium and cook for 10 minutes, stirring often.

The Plank
The plank is an exercise that works your entire core. To do it, just get down on the ground in a pushup position. This position has your hands and feet on the ground with your legs, arms, and back raised and flat as a board. Once you get there, hold the position as long as you can with proper form.

Serves 6

171 calories
5g fat
7g carbohydrates
25g protein
492mg sodium
1g fiber

Ingredients
1½ pounds top sirloin, cut in strips
1 clove fresh garlic, minced
4 tablespoons vinegar
½ cup green onions, sliced
½ teaspoon all-purpose seasoning
½ cup bell peppers, sliced
½ cup yellow onions, sliced
½ cup broccoli florets
½ cup carrot sticks
½ cup baby corn
1 tablespoon dry ginger or 2 tablespoons freshly ground ginger
¼ cup low-sodium soy sauce

Fiery Bombay Beef Curry

This Indian dish mixes individual spices to create a unique curry. Curry is a word used to describe any spiced sauce-based dishes cooked in various Asian styles.

1. Mix all ingredients in a large bowl. Pour ingredients in a large skillet coated with nonstick spray. Cook on medium high for 15 minutes, stirring often.

2. Cover and simmer for 15 minutes, stirring often.

Challenge Yourself
If you don't like running, try walking at an incline instead. You'll amp up the amount of calories you burn and add a killer glute, hamstring, and quadriceps workout as well. You can also go further or train for a longer period of time to increase the difficulty of your workout.

Serves 6

216 calories
10g fat
7g carbohydrates
24g protein
97mg sodium
2g fiber

Ingredients
1 clove fresh garlic, minced
1 cup onions, sliced
1 tablespoon green chilies, finely chopped
1 tablespoon ground ginger
2 teaspoons turmeric
1 teaspoon cumin
1 teaspoon coriander
1 teaspoon chili powder
½ teaspoon all-purpose seasoning
2 cups tomatoes, diced
½ cup coconut milk
1½ pounds top sirloin, in strips

Chapter 14
Seafood

Cumin and Coriander Crusted Mahi-Mahi

This delicious entrée combines vibrant cumin, coriander, and cilantro for a potent rub on the mahi-mahi filet. Salmon could also be flavored with this rub.

Serves 6

144 calories
3g fat
1g carbohydrates
26g protein
146mg sodium
0g fiber

Ingredients

1 tablespoon olive oil
1 clove fresh garlic, minced
½ teaspoon all-purpose
   seasoning
3 tablespoons fresh cilantro,
   finely chopped
2 tablespoons finely chopped
   onions
1 teaspoon cumin
½ teaspoon coriander
½ teaspoon black pepper
6 mahi-mahi fillets

1. Mix all ingredients expect mahi-mahi in a bowl to create a paste. Coat each fillet with paste.

2. Spray a 9" × 13" baking dish with nonstick spray. Place fillets in the dish without crowding and cover with foil.

3. Bake at 350°F for 10 minutes. Turn and bake uncovered for an additional 5 minutes or until fish flakes easily with a fork.

When Are Big Bellies Good?
It's never a good idea for pregnant women to try to keep their bellies flat. Let your belly grow for now, and you can train for flat abs again when Junior is safely in your arms!

Malaysian-Glazed Tilapia

Malaysian cuisine is known for utilizing fresh citrus juices and fruits and combining them with honey and rice vinegar to create refreshing flavors.

1. Mix all ingredients except tilapia in a bowl.

2. Spray a 9" × 13" baking dish with nonstick spray. Place tilapia fillets in the baking dish. Pour the mixture over the fish.

3. Bake at 350°F for 15 minutes or until fish flakes easily.

Race for a Flatter Belly
If you're having trouble exercising as frequently as you should, sign up for a race! Choose a race that you're not presently prepared to participate in and then officially sign up. Once you've paid the fee, you'll be more likely to force yourself into training for it and reaching that finish line!

Serves 6

189 calories
2g fat
8g carbohydrates
31g protein
128mg sodium
0g fiber

Ingredients
2 tablespoons freshly squeezed lemon juice
2 tablespoons freshly squeezed orange juice
2 teaspoons rice vinegar
2 tablespoons honey
1 clove fresh garlic, minced
2 teaspoons hoisin sauce
¼ cup green onions, sliced
½ teaspoon cornstarch
1 tablespoon olive oil
½ teaspoon chili powder
½ teaspoon all-purpose seasoning
6 tilapia fillets

Tilapia with Tomatoes and Olives

Tilapia is a mildly flavored fish. The olives and wine combination make this a great topping for fish, shrimp, or scallops.

1. Mix all ingredients except tilapia in a bowl and set aside.

2. Spray a 9" × 13" baking dish with nonstick spray. Place tilapia fillets in the dish. Pour mixture over the fish; cover with foil.

3. Bake at 350°F for 15 minutes or until fish flakes easily.

Serves 6

199 calories
4g fat
4g carbohydrates
31g protein
212mg sodium
1g fiber

Ingredients

1 tablespoon olive oil
1 clove fresh garlic, minced
½ teaspoon all-purpose seasoning
1½ cups diced tomatoes
½ cup green olives, halved
½ cup white cooking wine
¼ teaspoon black pepper
½ cup chopped onions
6 tilapia fillets

Salmon with Pineapple-Jalapeño Relish

Relish is typically a cooked vegetable or fruit item that is then used as a condiment. In this dish, the combination of pineapple, red onions, and jalapeño peppers creates a fiery and sweet topping for salmon.

1. Mix all ingredients except salmon fillets in a bowl.

2. Spray a 9" × 13" baking dish with nonstick spray. Place salmon in the dish. Pour mixture over the fish; cover with foil.

3. Bake at 350°F for 15 minutes or until fish flakes easily.

Serves 6

220 calories
5g fat
15g carbohydrates
29g protein
121mg sodium
1g fiber

Ingredients

1 clove fresh garlic, minced
½ teaspoon all-purpose seasoning
2 cups crushed pineapples
¼ chopped red onion
1 tablespoon freshly squeezed lemon juice
1 tablespoon sugar or Splenda
½ teaspoon jalapeño peppers, finely chopped
1 teaspoon chili powder
6 4- or 5-ounce salmon fillets

Honey Spicy Salmon

This recipe is fantastic if you substitute hard tofu for the salmon. This will make the recipe lower in fat but also lower in omega-3 and omega-6 fatty acids.

1. Mix all ingredients except salmon fillets in a bowl.

2. Spray a 9" × 13" baking dish with nonstick spray. Place salmon fillets in the dish. Pour mixture over the fish; cover with foil.

3. Bake at 350°F for 15 minutes or until fish flakes easily.

Good Fats

Although fat is usually considered a bad thing, it really is a necessary nutrient that you need each day. Fat is vital to brain function, cell protection, and energy storage. Fifteen percent of your caloric intake each day should be from sources of good fats like olives, nuts, avocados, canola oil, olive oil, salmon, sardines, and tuna.

Serves 6

206 calories
5g fat
11g carbohydrates
29g protein
474mg sodium
0g fiber

Ingredients

½ cup rice vinegar
3 tablespoons honey
2 tablespoons low-sodium soy sauce
1 teaspoon ground red pepper
½ teaspoon kosher salt
½ teaspoon five-spice powder
½ cup green onions, sliced
½ teaspoon all-purpose seasoning
1 clove fresh garlic, minced
6 4- or 5-ounce salmon fillets

Orange Teriyaki Salmon

Serves 6

201 calories
5g fat
9g carbohydrates
29g protein
316mg sodium
1g fiber

Ingredients

2 tablespoons low-sodium
    soy sauce
1 clove fresh garlic, minced
½ teaspoon all-purpose
    seasoning
1 tablespoon honey
1 tablespoon rice vinegar
3 tablespoons freshly
    squeezed orange juice
½ cup green onions, sliced
6 4- or 5-ounce salmon fillets
1 cup orange slices

This recipe creates its own teriyaki sauce, which makes for the perfect marinade when combined with fresh orange juice. This can also be used on beef or chicken.

1. Mix all ingredients except salmon fillets and orange slices in a bowl.

2. Spray a 9" × 13" baking dish with nonstick spray. Place salmon in the dish. Pour mixture over the fish and top with orange slices.

3. Cover with foil and bake at 350°F for 15 minutes or until fish flakes easily.

Charred Tilapia Fillets

These fillets could also be grilled and served with steamed or grilled vegetables or a baked sweet potato.

1. Spray a 9" × 13" baking dish with nonstick spray.

2. Mix all ingredients except tilapia fillets in a bowl. Coat tilapia with mixture. Place fillets in dish without crowding.

3. Bake at 380°F for 10 to 12 minutes or until fish flakes easily.

Brrrr!

Frigid temperatures are not an acceptable excuse for you to miss your workouts. If you must stay inside, use home fitness equipment or work out with videos. Another plan is to embrace the weather and try some winter sports. Cross country skiing, ice skating, and snowshoeing are excellent choices.

Serves 6

175 calories
2g fat
4g carbohydrates
31g protein
568mg sodium
0g fiber

Ingredients
1 tablespoon olive oil
1 clove fresh garlic, minced
½ teaspoon all-purpose
    seasoning
4 tablespoons low-sodium
    soy sauce
2 tablespoons Worcestershire
    sauce
2 teaspoons spicy mustard
2 teaspoons sugar or Splenda
2 teaspoons fresh parsley,
    finely chopped
6 tilapia fillets

Nutty Coated Salmon Steaks

Apple butter is a highly concentrated form of apple sauce. Its deep brown color comes from the caramelizing of the natural sugars in the apples.

Serves 6

207 calories
8g fat
3g carbohydrates
29g protein
149mg sodium
0g fiber

Ingredients
6 4- to 5-ounce salmon steaks
1 tablespoon apple butter
1 clove fresh garlic, minced
½ teaspoon all-purpose
    seasoning
1 tablespoon spicy mustard
¼ teaspoon dried thyme
¼ cup chopped pecans

1. Spray a 9" × 13" baking dish with cooking spray. Place salmon steaks in the dish.

2. Mix apple butter, garlic, all-purpose seasoning, mustard, and thyme. Spoon mixture over salmon. Top with chopped pecans.

3. Bake at 365°F for 15 minutes or until fish flakes easily.

Orange Roughy with Parsley Sauce

Orange roughy is a firm fish with a mild flavor. It is perfect for grilling. In this recipe tuna or mahi-mahi fillets could be substituted for the orange roughy.

Serves 6

131 calories
2g fat
4g carbohydrates
23g protein
154mg sodium
0g fiber

Ingredients
1 teaspoon olive oil
2 tablespoons fresh parsley,
    chopped
1 clove fresh garlic, minced
½ teaspoon all-purpose
    seasoning
4 teaspoons Smart Squeeze
1 cup skim milk
1 cup yellow onion slices
¼ cup low-sodium chicken
    broth
6 orange roughy fillets

Spray a nonstick skillet with cooking spray. In a bowl, mix all ingredients except fish. Place fish in skillet and pour mixture over. Cook on medium heat for 8 to 10 minutes. Simmer for 5 minutes or until fish flakes easily and sauce thickens.

Baked Tilapia with Citrus and Herbs

The ancient Greeks and Romans related thyme with courage, vigor, and strength. Whenever you add thyme, remind yourself to work out and grow stronger.

1. Mix all ingredients except tilapia fillets in a bowl.

2. Spray a 9" × 13" baking dish with nonstick spray. Place tilapia fillets in the dish. Pour mixture over the fish; cover with foil.

3. Bake at 350°F for 15 minutes or until fish flakes easily.

Stretching for Strength
When it comes to weight loss, strength training and cardiovascular exercise rank as top priorities. Surprisingly, stretching can be equally important. Why? Because it keeps your muscles pliable, alleviates soreness, and ultimately prevents injuries. Train for flexibility on a regular basis, and you'll be more likely to continue with vigorous exercise for a long time.

Serves 6

150 calories
1g fat
2g carbohydrates
31g protein
254mg sodium
1g fiber

Ingredients
2 tablespoons freshly squeezed lemon juice
1 clove fresh garlic, minced
½ teaspoon all-purpose seasoning
2 teaspoons fresh parsley, chopped
2 teaspoons dried thyme
1 teaspoon lemon grind
½ teaspoon sea salt
1 teaspoon olive oil
6 5-ounce tilapia fillets

Mom's Tuna Salad

This is a recipe you could whip up on a weekend afternoon to feed the whole family quickly. It takes less than 10 minutes to make!

Combine all ingredients in a large bowl, varying the amount of mayonnaise depending on how moist you like your tuna salad.

Expert Opinion on Tuna
90 percent of all bodybuilders and fitness competitors in the world will tell you they make a habit of feasting on tuna. They know it's an excellent source of protein, and it offers very few calories and almost no fat. These people need to be lean to compete, and tuna is often their answer.

Serves 1

224 calories
1g fat
15g carbohydrates
37g protein
1,247mg sodium
1g fiber

Ingredients
1 large can white tuna in water, chopped
2 tablespoons yellow onions, diced
2 tablespoons bell peppers, diced
1 tablespoon celery stalk, diced
¼ cup fat-free mayonnaise
Salt and pepper to taste

Simply Boiled Shrimp

Placing the boiled shrimp in cold water preserves a crunchy texture on the outside but leaves the inside tender.

Add shrimp and Old Bay to a large pot of boiling water and boil for about 3 minutes or until shrimp look bright pink. Remove quickly from pot and quickly place in cold water.

Serves 4

241 calories
4g fat
2g carbohydrates
46g protein
385mg sodium
0g fiber

Ingredients
2 pounds peeled shrimp
1 tablespoon Old Bay

Cilantro Citrus Caribbean Mahi-Mahi

Adding any type of citrus fruit or juice to any seafood dish will tremendously reduce the "fishy" smell and flavor.

1. Coat a large skillet with nonstick spray. Mix all ingredients except fish, lemon slices, and orange slices. Add fish to skillet, coat with mixture, and top with lemon and orange slices.

2. Cover and cook on medium heat for 15 to 20 minutes or until fish flakes easily.

Lose the Love Handles

Contrary to popular belief, love handles cannot be banished with side bends. Love handles are pockets of fat, and just like any other fatty area on your body, they can only be destroyed by burning more calories than you consume. Overall fat loss is the key to getting rid of love handles, belly fat, and man boobs.

Serves 6

160 calories
3g fat
5g carbohydrates
27g protein
147mg sodium
1g fiber

Ingredients

1 tablespoon olive oil
1 clove fresh garlic, minced
½ teaspoon all-purpose seasoning
½ cup yellow onions, sliced
½ cup cilantro, chopped
2 teaspoons parsley, chopped
¼ cup freshly squeezed orange juice
¼ cup freshly squeezed lemon juice
½ teaspoon cumin
6 3- to 5-ounce mahi-mahi fillets
¼ cup lemon slices
¼ cup orange slices

Festive Scallops

This dish goes great when served over steamed broccoli. The term "festive"
comes from the colorful and flavorful combination of ingredients.

Serves 6

205 calories
2g fat
20g carbohydrates
22g protein
772mg sodium
3g fiber

Ingredients

1 cup bell peppers, diced
2 cups tomatoes, diced
2 tablespoons cilantro,
  chopped
½ teaspoon all-purpose
  seasoning
1 clove fresh garlic, minced
2 cups vegetable broth
½ cup cooking wine
1 cup carrots, chopped
1 teaspoon oregano
1 cup yellow onions, sliced
1½ pounds scallops, cleaned

1. Coat a deep skillet with nonstick spray. Add all ingredients except scallops. Cook on medium high for 5 to 8 minutes, stirring often.

2. Add scallops to skillet, cover, and simmer for 10 minutes, stirring often.

Money Management
Some people feel guilty for spending money on health club memberships and fitness tools, but they are smart investments in the long run. Just think about how much money you might spend on junk food, alcohol, doctor appointments, and prescriptions if you weren't more vigilant about your health.

Roasted Shrimp Provençal

The shrimp in this recipe could be substituted by scallops or any mild flavor fish, such as tilapia or mahi-mahi. Serve this recipe with mixed garden vegetables.

Spray a 9" × 13" baking dish with nonstick spray. Mix all ingredients together in a large bowl. Pour mixture into the dish. Roast at 385°F for 15 to 20 minutes.

Serves 6

163 calories
4g fat
3g carbohydrates
23g protein
202mg sodium
0g fiber

Ingredients

1 tablespoon olive oil
1 clove fresh garlic, minced
1 tablespoon Italian herbs
1 tablespoon freshly squeezed lemon juice
½ teaspoon kosher salt
½ teaspoon black pepper
½ cup white onion, finely chopped
¼ cup white wine
½ teaspoon all-purpose seasoning
1½ pounds shrimp, peeled and deveined

Mediterranean-Style Shrimp

201 calories
4g fat
15g carbohydrates
25g protein
549mg sodium
2g fiber

Ingredients

1½ pounds shrimp, peeled
    and deveined
1 clove fresh garlic, minced
½ teaspoon all-purpose
    seasoning
¼ cup freshly squeezed lemon
    juice
1 teaspoon thyme
2 tablespoons capers
½ teaspoon olive oil
½ cup white onions, chopped
2 cups marinara sauce
4 cups Spaghetti Squash,
    cooked (page 135)

Shrimp is a very healthy option, but it's incredible how often people destroy the healthfulness of it. Avoid fried shrimp and shrimp scampi. The first is deep-fried and the second is drenched in butter.

1. Coat a skillet with nonstick spray. Add all ingredients except marinara and spaghetti squash to skillet. Sauté on medium heat for 7 minutes, stirring often.

2. Add marinara sauce to skillet and simmer for 8 minutes, stirring often. Serve over spaghetti squash.

Swimsuits in December

It's amazing how many people neglect their weight throughout the winter because they're able to cover up most of the time due to chilly weather. It's no fun to have to recover from that by dieting for spring. Instead, make a habit of tossing on your swimsuit every two weeks throughout the winter; this reality check will keep you on task.

Chapter 15
Not-So-Sinful Desserts

Fitz's Ultimate Low-Fat Chocolate Chip Cookies

Serves 12

122 calories
3g fat
21g carbohydrates
1g protein
87mg sodium
0g fiber

Ingredients
*Betty Crocker Chocolate Chip
    Cookie Mix*
¼ cup Egg Beaters
*½ cup Smart Squeeze or ½
    cup sugar-free vanilla-
    flavored syrup*

*Do not use the ingredients suggested on the cookie mix packaging! The
ingredients in this recipe are designed to replace the ones used in the original
recipe.*

1. Preheat oven to 350°F. Coat two large cookie sheets with nonstick
    spray and set aside.

2. Mix all ingredients in a large bowl with a fork until moist and smooth.
    Using a teaspoon, drop cookie dough onto sheets without crowding.

3. Bake for 8 to 10 minutes.

Sneaky Fun
*These cookies are completely deceptive. No one in the world would ever
believe they are low in fat. In fact, it might be fun for you to serve them to
your friends and family and wait until the raves come in to tell them that
they're really a healthier version of original chocolate chip cookies.*

Apple-Strawberry Crumble

You can tell a banana is ripe when the skin turns a dark yellow. Bananas that are still green are not as sweet and are quite firm.

1. Combine apples and strawberries and pour into a baking dish. Combine other ingredients except whipped cream and pile on top of the fruit.

2. Bake at 350°F for 10 to 15 minutes, or until golden brown and bubbling. Top with a squirt of fat-free whipped cream.

How to Peel an Apple
Start by holding the apple steady on a cutting board. Use a vegetable peeler to remove the skin by pushing the peeler away from you, top to bottom. Turn and peel the apple until it's bare. The apple peel is full of fiber, so keep it if you can!

Serves 4

233 calories
2g fat
47g carbohydrates
5g protein
228mg sodium
6g fiber

Ingredients
2 cups green apples, peeled and chopped
2 cups strawberries, chopped
¼ cup Egg Beaters
1 mashed ripe banana
1 cup oatmeal
¼ cup Splenda brown sugar
½ teaspoon cinnamon
Fat-free whipped cream to top

Fitz's Raspberry Yum Yum Cake

For a healthier dessert, use the ingredients in this recipe to replace the ones used in the recipe on the box. Top your cake with Fat-Free Cream Cheese Frosting (page 269).

Serves 12

331 calories
7g fat
63g carbohydrates
4g protein
512mg sodium
3g fiber

Ingredients
*1 box Betty Crocker
    SuperMoist White Cake
    Mix
1/3 cup Smart Squeeze or 1/3
    cup sugar-free vanilla-
    flavored syrup
½ cup Egg Beaters
18 ounces fresh raspberries*

1. Preheat oven to 350°F.

2. Combine cake mix, Smart Squeeze, and Egg Beaters in a large bowl; stir until smooth. Pour half of cake batter into an 8" round pan. Bake for 5 minutes.

3. Remove from oven and spread ⅔ of raspberries evenly over partially cooked cake batter. Cover raspberries with remaining cake batter and return to oven.

4. Bake for another 20 to 25 minutes or until a toothpick inserted in the center comes out clean. Cool the cake and invert it onto a dish.

5. Frost if desired, cover with remaining raspberries, and serve.

Creating a Supportive Base
The reason for cooking the first half of the cake batter for a few minutes is to prevent the raspberries from sinking to the bottom of the pan. The cooking time creates just enough opportunity for the cake batter to become firm enough to support the weight of the berries.

Crooked Choco-Chip Banana Cake

*The only thing missing from unsweetened applesauce is several scoops of sugar!
The flavors are almost identical, so save the calories and always choose the
unsweetened variety.*

1. Preheat oven to 350°F.

2. Combine flour, baking powder, baking soda, Splenda, salt, and chocolate chips in a large bowl and stir well. Add remaining ingredients; stir until smooth.

3. Pour batter into an 8" square pan. Bake for 30 minutes. Cool and cut into nine squares.

Daily Dairy

Dairy is packed with calcium and vitamin D. For a lean body, getting calcium from sources such as yogurt, low-fat cheeses, and dark leafy greens is a smarter choice. A tall glass of skim milk is healthy, but it will still leave you hungry. Choose chewable calcium sources and you'll consume fewer calories throughout your day.

Serves 9

163 calories
4g fat
33g carbohydrates
5g protein
146mg sodium
3g fiber

Ingredients

¾ cup whole wheat flour
¾ cup all-purpose flour
1 teaspoon baking powder
¼ teaspoon baking soda
1/8 teaspoon salt
2/3 cup dark chocolate chips
¾ cup Splenda
2/3 cup mashed ripe bananas
1/3 cup unsweetened
    applesauce
1/3 cup fat-free plain yogurt
½ cup Egg Beaters
1 teaspoon banana extract

Low-Fat Pineapple Upside-Down Cake

This is still a cake, but it's a great idea to base desserts around fruit. Eventually you'll start to lean on fruit alone and forget about the cake!

1. Preheat oven to 350°F. Coat two 9" round pans with nonstick spray and set aside.

2. In a large bowl, combine cake mix, water, Smart Squeeze, and Egg Beaters.

3. Beat mixture on low speed for 2 minutes or until batter is moist and smooth.

4. Sprinkle Splenda on bottom of one cake pan. Place pineapple slices on top of Splenda. Pour cake batter evenly between both pans.

5. Bake cakes for 31 minutes or until a toothpick inserted in the center comes out clean. Allow cakes to cool. Invert cake without pineapple topping onto a dish.

6. Scoop 5 tablespoons of Cool Whip onto cake in dish. Invert second cake on top of first cake and top with another 5 tablespoons of Cool Whip.

Defying Your Desserts
It can be hard to resist eating batter while baking cakes, cookies, or brownies. A simple way to help yourself refuse the temptation while you bake is to suck on a peppermint. The strong minty flavor will take the enjoyment out of licking the bowl. If you don't have a mint, brush your teeth!

Fat-Free Cream Cheese Frosting

Multiply these ingredients depending on how much you need.

Blend ingredients in a mixer at low speed. Chill at least 15 minutes and frost any dessert!

Serves 12

19 calories
0g fat
3g carbohydrates
3g protein
103mg sodium
0g fiber

Ingredients
1 8-ounce package fat-free cream cheese
1/3 cup Splenda
1 teaspoon vanilla

Sweet Ricotta Dessert

Instead of crawling into bed with a big bowl of ice cream, try this. It's sweet and creamy like ice cream, but it's far lower in calories and the high protein content will actually fill you up!

Combine ingredients in a bowl, stir well, and enjoy!

Serves 1

51 calories
0g fat
4g carbohydrates
9g protein
120mg sodium
0g fiber

Ingredients
¼ cup fat-free ricotta cheese
½ teaspoon vanilla extract
1 teaspoon Splenda

Low-Fat Key Lime Pie

Serves 8

307 calories
7g fat
55g carbohydrates
8g protein
270mg sodium
1g fiber

Ingredients
½ cup Egg Beaters
½ cup Key lime juice
1 14-ounce can fat-free
    condensed milk
4 egg whites
½ teaspoon cream of tartar
½ cup Splenda
1 preprepared graham
    cracker crust

Premade graham cracker crusts are sold at most grocery stores and make pie-making much more doable.

1. Preheat oven to 350°F.

2. In a medium mixing bowl, mix Egg Beaters, Key lime juice, and fat-free condensed milk for filling.

3. In a small mixing bowl, beat egg whites and cream of tartar until peaks form. Slowly beat in Splenda until stiff but not dry to form the meringue.

4. Fold ¼ of the meringue into pie filling. Pour into pie shell. Spread remaining meringue on top of pie, extending to the edge of the shell.

5. Bake for 12 to 15 minutes or until golden brown. Cool and chill well before serving.

Resident Key Limes
Key limes are a unique breed of limes often as small as a ping-pong ball or as large as a golf ball. They are also incredibly aromatic, which makes them a delight in the kitchen. Key limes are not indigenous to the Florida Keys, but they've earned their resident status.

Jacki's Sugar-Free Strawberry Pie

Have fun changing up the flavor by trying different fruits like peaches or various flavors of sugar-free gelatin.

1. Bake pie shell and let cool.

2. Add water, cornstarch, and boxes of gelatin to a large saucepan. Stir constantly until it boils and cook for 1 minute. Cool to room temperature.

3. Add strawberries to gelatin, then mix and pour into pie shell. Refrigerate 2 hours.

Healthy Birthday Bash
This pie is festive yet not overly fattening like traditional cake. Stick some candles in it and try some other healthy alternatives. Stick with fruit and veggie platters, baked chips, and low-fat dips for appetizers. Serve lean meats with healthy salads for a meal. Fill piñatas with toys instead of candy.

Serves 8

145 calories
6g fat
20g carbohydrates
2g protein
161mg sodium
3g fiber

Ingredients
*9" pie shell
3 cups water
3 rounded tablespoons
    cornstarch
2 3-ounce boxes sugar-free
    strawberry gelatin
2 pounds fresh strawberries,
    chopped*

Low-Fat Super Chunky Chocolate Brownies

Serves 12

48 calories
0g fat
10g carbohydrates
1g protein
30mg sodium
0g fiber

Ingredients
*1 box Betty Crocker Hershey's
Triple Chunk Supreme
Brownie Mix*
½ cup Egg Beaters
*½ cup sugar-free chocolate
syrup*
3 tablespoons water

The ingredients listed in this recipe are designed to provide a healthier dessert, so disregard the ingredients on the box.

1. Coat a 9" × 13" baking dish with nonstick spray.

2. Stir brownie mix, Egg Beaters, syrup, and water together in a bowl. Blend well. Pour mix into baking dish.

3. Bake in oven at 350°F for 26 to 28 minutes.

Taming Temptations
A smart rule of thumb for baking desserts is to only bake when you're able to give the bulk of your treats away. Even if you're baking low-fat cookies or cakes, they still account for extra calories. Leaving temptation on the counter is unfair to your efforts. Bake some goodies, enjoy one, and give the rest away.

Fitz's Low-Fat Cheesecake

This is a basic fat-free cheesecake recipe, so build on it to create your own tasty treats. Try out various flavors of extracts and add unique ingredients like graham cracker bits, pretzel pieces, fruit, and small bits of dark chocolate.

1. In an electric mixer, combine cream cheese, Splenda, and vanilla on medium speed. Add Egg Beaters and mix until well blended. Pour mixture into crust.

2. Bake at 350°F for 40 minutes or until center is almost set. Cool and refrigerate for 2 hours or overnight.

Bake the Bad Stuff
If you're hell-bent on baking goodies for an occasion but you really don't want to indulge, bake something you don't enjoy. If you despise peanut butter, make peanut butter cookies. Hate Key lime pie? Make it! You'll still contribute to the event, and you will be able to maintain your fitness program.

Serves 8

240 calories
9g fat
29g carbohydrates
15g protein
666mg sodium
0g fiber

Ingredients
*3 8-ounce packages fat-free
    cream cheese, softened*
¾ cup Splenda
1 teaspoon vanilla extract
¾ cup Egg Beaters
*1 prepared low-fat graham
    cracker crust*

Serves 10

259 calories
9g fat
33g carbohydrates
13g protein
517mg sodium
1g fiber

Ingredients

3 8-ounce packages fat-free
    cream cheese, softened
¾ cup Splenda
1 teaspoon vanilla extract
¾ cup Egg Beaters
½ cup dark chocolate morsels
½ cup all-purpose flour
1 prepared low-fat graham
    cracker crust

Darn Low-Fat Chocolate Chip Cheesecake

This low-fat delight is great for a party.

1. In an electric mixer, combine cream cheese, Splenda, and vanilla on medium speed. Add Egg Beaters and mix until well blended.

2. In a separate bowl, lightly coat chocolate morsels with flour. Gently fold chocolate morsels into cream cheese mixture and pour into the crust.

3. Bake at 350°F for 40 minutes or until center is almost set. Cool and refrigerate for 2 hours or overnight.

DIY Graham Cracker Crust

To make your own low-fat pie crust, coat a pie pan with nonstick spray, crush 12 ounces of graham crackers in a plastic bag, mix the crumbs with ¼ cup Egg Beaters, and spread onto the pan. Bake for 5 minutes in the oven before adding the cheesecake mix.

Darn Low-Fat Raspberry Cheesecake

These raspberries are a very rich and flavorful addition to the creamy cheesecake texture. Blueberries and strawberries also make amazing choices.

1. In an electric mixer, combine cream cheese, Splenda, and vanilla on medium speed. Add Egg Beaters and mix until well blended.

2. Gently fold raspberries into mixture. Pour mixture into crust. Bake at 350°F for 40 minutes or until center is almost set.

3. Cool and refrigerate for 2 hours or overnight.

Freezing Fruit
When your fruit hits a state of extreme ripeness, throw it in the freezer instead of throwing it out. Produce often goes bad before you can eat it. Freeze what you can't enjoy fresh and add it to smoothies or yogurt at a later date.

Serves 8

238 calories
8g fat
31g carbohydrates
15g protein
645mg sodium
1g fiber

Ingredients
3 8-ounce packages fat-free cream cheese, softened
¾ cup Splenda
1 teaspoon vanilla extract
¾ cup Egg Beaters
1½ cups frozen raspberries
1 prepared low-fat graham cracker crust

Ras-Blueberry Smoothie

The combination of raspberries and blueberries creates a very intense flavor. For a milder taste, add ½ cup of plain fat-free yogurt to the blender.

Blend all ingredients in blender until smooth. Serve immediately.

Serves 4

219 calories
1g fat
52g carbohydrates
4g protein
34mg sodium
8g fiber

Ingredients

2 cups frozen raspberries
2 cups frozen blueberries
1 cup freshly squeezed
    orange juice
1 cup skim milk
½ teaspoon vanilla extract
Handful ice

Strawberry, Blueberry, and Banana Smoothie

If you freeze these smoothies, you can eat them with a spoon or off of a stick like you would ice cream.

Blend all ingredients in blender until smooth. Serve immediately.

Serves 4

99 calories
1g fat
21g carbohydrates
3g protein
33mg sodium
2g fiber

Ingredients

1 cup frozen strawberries,
    leaves removed
½ cup frozen blueberries
1 frozen banana
1 cup freshly squeezed
    orange juice
1 cup skim milk
½ teaspoon vanilla extract
Handful ice

Raspberry-Pineapple Smoothie

This tropical treat will make a splash at your luau or pool party. Forget the alcohol and cake altogether and serve this smoothie as a treat.

Blend all ingredients in blender until smooth. Serve immediately.

Can You Can-Can?
The benefit of using canned produce is clear. You can buy it one day and use it many months later. This convenience can be a great thing! Unfortunately, canned fruits and vegetables are often packed in sugar-laden syrups that crank the calorie count way up. To avoid this, simply look for the terms "no-sugar added" or "packed in natural juices."

Serves 4

214 calories
0g fat
51g carbohydrates
4g protein
34mg sodium
6g fiber

Ingredients
*2 cups frozen raspberries
1 8-ounce can crushed
    pineapples (with natural
    juices)
1 cup freshly squeezed
    orange juice
1 cup skim milk
½ teaspoon vanilla extract
Handful ice*

Strawberry Smoothie

The yogurt in this smoothie gives the strawberries a very soft and creamy flavor. It's also filled with vitamin C. Serve this pink treat to your love on Valentine's Day.

Blend all ingredients in blender until smooth. Serve immediately.

Serves 4

216 calories
1g fat
52g carbohydrates
5g protein
56mg sodium
4g fiber

Ingredients
*3 cups frozen strawberries,
    leaves removed
1 cup freshly squeezed
    orange juice
1 cup skim milk
½ cup fat-free plain yogurt
½ teaspoon vanilla extract
Handful ice*

Creamy Blueberry Smoothie

A study out of Britain's University of Reading found that those who downed these baby blues were successful at fighting stage fright.

Blend all ingredients in blender until smooth. Serve immediately.

Serves 4

118 calories
1g fat
26g carbohydrates
3g protein
33mg sodium
3g fiber

Ingredients
2 cups frozen blueberries
1 frozen banana
*1 cup freshly squeezed
    orange juice*
1 cup skim milk
½ teaspoon vanilla extract
Handful ice

Strawberry-Kiwi Smoothie

Kiwifruits offer a grand amount of vitamin C and potassium (almost as much as a banana), and they even contain omega-3 fatty acids. Kiwi is also a very good source of fiber, which is helpful in lowering cholesterol and maintaining a healthy colon.

Blend all ingredients in blender until smooth. Serve immediately.

Serves 4

177 calories
1g fat
43g carbohydrates
4g protein
36mg sodium
4g fiber

Ingredients
*2 cups frozen strawberries,
    leaves removed*
1 cup frozen kiwi
*1 cup freshly squeezed
    orange juice*
1 cup skim milk
½ teaspoon vanilla extract
Handful ice

Banana Smoothie

The benefits of eating fresh produce are endless; they far outweigh the downsides.

Blend all ingredients in blender until smooth. Serve immediately.

Gaga for Bananas
Bananas are the perfect food for the little ones. They're sweet, soft, and full of nutrition. In fact, many parents use the banana as a first food. Share a Banana Smoothie with your teeny tot; it's a much better choice than ice cream and a healthy opportunity for you both!

Serves 4

132 calories
1g fat
30g carbohydrates
3g protein
33mg sodium
2g fiber

Ingredients
3 frozen bananas
1 cup freshly squeezed orange juice
1 cup skim milk
½ teaspoon vanilla extract
Handful ice

Peaches, Strawberries, and Banana Smoothie

Use fresh slices of fruit to garnish your finished smoothie and add a little substance to your dessert.

Blend all ingredients in blender until smooth. Serve immediately.

How to Make Fresh Orange Juice
Wash and halve oranges. Cut circularly inside the orange peel, slightly releasing the fruit. Grip orange and squeeze directly into a glass. Squeeze the orange at various angles until no more juice comes out. Strain your juice to remove pulp if you prefer.

Serves 4

186 calories
1g fat
45g carbohydrates
4g protein
37mg sodium
3g fiber

Ingredients
1 cup frozen strawberries, leaves removed
1 cup frozen peeled peach slices
1 frozen banana
1 cup freshly squeezed orange juice
1 cup skim milk
½ teaspoon vanilla extract
Handful ice

Peaches and Cream Smoothie

If you don't have fat-free plain yogurt in your fridge, use another flavor instead.

Blend all ingredients in blender until smooth. Serve immediately.

Protective Gear

Make sure you're always wearing proper protective gear for all of your workouts. Sneakers, knee pads, helmets, cups, and other safety equipment are designed to keep you in the game. Slacking off on your safety measures could land you in the emergency room. This mistake will force you into recovery and keep you from progressing toward your fitness goals.

Very Berry Smoothie

You can alter the amount of each berry you use in this smoothie to create fun colors. Make a variety and serve them in clear glasses for a beautiful effect!

Blend all ingredients in blender until smooth. Serve immediately.

Cranberry and Banana Smoothie

If you're prone to urinary tract infections, make this smoothie your go-to treat!
Cranberries are known to inhibit the growth of the bacteria that cause UTIs.

Blend all ingredients in blender until smooth. Serve immediately.

Serves 4

144 calories
1g fat
32g carbohydrates
5g protein
55mg sodium
4g fiber

Ingredients
2 cups frozen cranberries
2 frozen bananas
1 cup freshly squeezed
orange juice
1 cup skim milk
½ teaspoon vanilla extract
½ cup fat-free plain yogurt

The Pool Rules!

Even if you're not a great swimmer, you can still get a tremendous workout in the pool. In waist- to chest-deep water, walking, jogging, treading water, martial arts, and dancing are great ways to burn calories with little impact. For strength training in the pool, try the high-tech equipment from Aqualogix.

Orange Smoothie

This smoothie may remind you of your cool days roaming through the mall sipping on an Orange Julius.

Blend all ingredients in blender until smooth. Serve immediately.

Serves 4

150 calories
1g fat
32g carbohydrates
5g protein
55mg sodium
1g fiber

Ingredients
3 cups frozen freshly
squeezed orange juice
1 frozen banana
1 cup skim milk
½ teaspoon vanilla extract
½ cup fat-free plain yogurt

Strawberry-Pineapple Smoothie

Bring the tropics into your backyard with this exotic smoothie.

Blend all ingredients well in blender until smooth. Serve immediately.

How to Peel and Cut a Pineapple
Use a serrated knife to cut the top and bottom off of the pineapple. Slice the sides off, following the curve of the fruit. Remove any remaining eyes and cut straight through the core from top to bottom. Cut around the core and slice the remaining fruit.

Pumpkin and Banana Smoothie

Pumpkins may be seasonal, but you can enjoy this tasty smoothie all year round.

Blend all ingredients in blender until smooth. Serve immediately.

Fitness on a Budget
If you don't have room in your budget for a health club membership or even a variety of fitness DVDs, fear not! Spend $20 on an expandable pullup bar for a door frame in your house and do those. Complement your pullups with pushups, dips on the floor, squats, lunges, and jogging and you'll be in great shape!

Serves 4

225 calories
1g fat
54g carbohydrates
5g protein
56mg sodium
4g fiber

Ingredients
2½ cups frozen strawberries,
    leafs removed
1 8-ounce can crushed
    pineapples (with natural
    juices)
1 cup freshly squeezed
    orange juice
1 cup skim milk
½ teaspoon vanilla extract
½ cup fat-free plain yogurt

Serves 4

191 calories
1g fat
41g carbohydrates
7g protein
84mg sodium
4g fiber

Ingredients
2 cups fat-free vanilla yogurt
1½ cups canned pumpkin,
    chilled
Handful ice
2/3 cup freshly squeezed
    orange juice
1 tablespoon Splenda brown
    sugar
1 teaspoon cinnamon
¼ teaspoon nutmeg
1 frozen ripe banana

Appendix A
Caloric Content of Beverages

All drinks are labeled for 8-ounce servings unless otherwise noted.

Beverage	Calories
Alcohol: 100 proof	669
Alcohol: 90 proof	596
Alcohol: 86 proof	565
Alcohol: 80 proof	524
Apple cider	95
Apple juice	95
Beer (Budweiser)	98
Beer (Bud Light)	72
Bloody Mary	177
Buttermilk	91
Chocolate milk, skim	79
Chocolate milk, 2%	163
Chocolate milk, whole	188
Club soda	0
Coconut milk	522
Coffee, black	2
Coffee liqueur	762
Coffee, with cream	48
Coffee, with cream and sugar	91
Cola	97
Cranberry-apple juice drink	152
Cranberry juice cocktail	132
Cream soda	98
Crème de menthe	841
Daiquiri	422
Dasani (fruit-flavored water)	1

Beverage	Calories
Diet soda	0
Eggnog	306
Fresca	2
Fruit punch	107
Full Throttle Original Energy Drink	220
Full Throttle Zero	5
Gatorade	50
Gatorade G2	25
Gin and tonic	172
Ginger ale	70
Grape juice	138
Grape soda	98
Grapefruit juice, canned and sweetened	104
Grapefruit juice, freshly squeezed	88
Hot cocoa	197
Kahlua	762
Lemon-lime soda	108
Lemon juice, freshly squeezed	57
Lemonade	100
Lime juice, freshly squeezed	61
Limeade	93
Manhattan	508
Martini	506
Milk, skim	79
Milk, 1%	102
Milk, 2%	113

Beverage	Calories
Milk, whole	145
Milk, goat whole	156
Milk, sheep whole	245
Milkshake, chocolate	270
Milkshake, strawberry	256
Milkshake, vanilla	254
Orange juice, freshly squeezed	102
Orange soda	109
Piña colada	422
Pineapple-orange juice drink	122
Pineapple juice	127
Powerade	65
Powerade Zero	0
Propel Fitness Water	10
Prune juice	161
Red Bull	100
Red Bull, sugar free	10
Root beer	93
Screwdriver	186
Starbucks Caffe Latte with 2% milk	100
Starbucks Cappuccino with 2% milk	80
Starbucks Espresso	5
Starbucks Caramel Frappuccino *(12 ounce with whipped cream)*	300
Starbucks Mocha Frappuccino *(12 ounce no whipped cream)*	280
Starbucks Lemonade Blended Beverage	125
Starbucks Tazo Chai Tea Latte	100
Tangerine juice	98
Tangelo juice	93
Tea, unsweetened	2
Tea, sweetened	77
Tea, low-cal instant	5
Tequila Sunrise	249

Beverage	Calories
Tom Collins	125
Tomato juice	39
Tonic water	77
Vegetable juice cocktail	43
Vodka martini	506
Water	0
Whiskey sour	308
Wine, dessert	311
Wine, red	163
Wine, rose	161
Wine, white	154

Appendix B
Smart Substitutions

Bagel	English muffin
Bread	Light-wheat bread
Broth	Low-sodium broth
Butter	Smart Squeeze* by Smart Beat
Chicken broth	Low-sodium chicken broth
Chocolate syrup	Sugar-free chocolate syrup
Cream cheese	Fat-free cream cheese
Eggs	Egg Beaters
Honey mustard	Dijon mustard
Jelly	Sugar-free preserves or sugar-free jelly
Maple syrup	Sugar-free maple syrup
Mayonnaise	Fat-free mayonnaise
Oil for baking	Smart Squeeze or sugar-free vanilla coffee flavoring syrup**
Ricotta cheese	Fat-free ricotta cheese
Salad dressing	Fat-free salad dressing
Sour cream	Fat-free sour cream
Soy sauce	Low-sodium soy sauce
Strawberry syrup	Sugar-free strawberry syrup
Sugar	Splenda
Teriyaki	Low-sodium teriyaki

* Smart Squeeze Margarine by Smart Beat might be tricky to find. If you do not see the white bottle with the green top on your grocer's shelves you can do two things:

1. Speak to the grocer's manager and request that the manager order some for you. This is not unusual, and most grocers are happy to comply.
2. Check out the product locator at the Smart Balance website (*www.smartbalance.com*) to find a grocer in your area that carries Smart Squeeze.

** Sugar-free syrups are very popular for flavoring coffee. DaVinci Gourmet (*www.davincigourmet.com*) makes a variety of sugar-free flavors, as does Torani Syrups (*www.flavoredsyrups.net*). When baking with these syrups, substitute equal portions of the syrups instead of using butter and oil.

Index

Note: Page numbers in **bold** indicate recipe category lists.

The EVERYTHING Series!

BUSINESS & PERSONAL FINANCE

Everything® Accounting Book
Everything® Budgeting Book, 2nd Ed.
Everything® Business Planning Book
Everything® Coaching and Mentoring Book, 2nd Ed.
Everything® Fundraising Book
Everything® Get Out of Debt Book
Everything® Grant Writing Book, 2nd Ed.
Everything® Guide to Buying Foreclosures
Everything® Guide to Fundraising, $15.95
Everything® Guide to Mortgages
Everything® Guide to Personal Finance for Single Mothers
Everything® Home-Based Business Book, 2nd Ed.
Everything® Homebuying Book, 3rd Ed., $15.95
Everything® Homeselling Book, 2nd Ed.
Everything® Human Resource Management Book
Everything® Improve Your Credit Book
Everything® Investing Book, 2nd Ed.
Everything® Landlording Book
Everything® Leadership Book, 2nd Ed.
Everything® Managing People Book, 2nd Ed.
Everything® Negotiating Book
Everything® Online Auctions Book
Everything® Online Business Book
Everything® Personal Finance Book
Everything® Personal Finance in Your 20s & 30s Book, 2nd Ed.
Everything® Personal Finance in Your 40s & 50s Book, $15.95
Everything® Project Management Book, 2nd Ed.
Everything® Real Estate Investing Book
Everything® Retirement Planning Book
Everything® Robert's Rules Book, $7.95
Everything® Selling Book
Everything® Start Your Own Business Book, 2nd Ed.
Everything® Wills & Estate Planning Book

COOKING

Everything® Barbecue Cookbook
Everything® Bartender's Book, 2nd Ed., $9.95
Everything® Calorie Counting Cookbook
Everything® Cheese Book
Everything® Chinese Cookbook
Everything® Classic Recipes Book
Everything® Cocktail Parties & Drinks Book
Everything® College Cookbook
Everything® Cooking for Baby and Toddler Book
Everything® Diabetes Cookbook
Everything® Easy Gourmet Cookbook
Everything® Fondue Cookbook
Everything® Food Allergy Cookbook, $15.95
Everything® Fondue Party Book
Everything® Gluten-Free Cookbook
Everything® Glycemic Index Cookbook
Everything® Grilling Cookbook
Everything® Healthy Cooking for Parties Book, $15.95
Everything® Holiday Cookbook
Everything® Indian Cookbook
Everything® Lactose-Free Cookbook
Everything® Low-Cholesterol Cookbook

Everything® Low-Fat High-Flavor Cookbook, 2nd Ed., $15.95
Everything® Low-Salt Cookbook
Everything® Meals for a Month Cookbook
Everything® Meals on a Budget Cookbook
Everything® Mediterranean Cookbook
Everything® Mexican Cookbook
Everything® No Trans Fat Cookbook
Everything® One-Pot Cookbook, 2nd Ed., $15.95
Everything® Organic Cooking for Baby & Toddler Book, $15.95
Everything® Pizza Cookbook
Everything® Quick Meals Cookbook, 2nd Ed., $15.95
Everything® Slow Cooker Cookbook
Everything® Slow Cooking for a Crowd Cookbook
Everything® Soup Cookbook
Everything® Stir-Fry Cookbook
Everything® Sugar-Free Cookbook
Everything® Tapas and Small Plates Cookbook
Everything® Tex-Mex Cookbook
Everything® Thai Cookbook
Everything® Vegetarian Cookbook
Everything® Whole-Grain, High-Fiber Cookbook
Everything® Wild Game Cookbook
Everything® Wine Book, 2nd Ed.

GAMES

Everything® 15-Minute Sudoku Book, $9.95
Everything® 30-Minute Sudoku Book, $9.95
Everything® Bible Crosswords Book, $9.95
Everything® Blackjack Strategy Book
Everything® Brain Strain Book, $9.95
Everything® Bridge Book
Everything® Card Games Book
Everything® Card Tricks Book, $9.95
Everything® Casino Gambling Book, 2nd Ed.
Everything® Chess Basics Book
Everything® Christmas Crosswords Book, $9.95
Everything® Craps Strategy Book
Everything® Crossword and Puzzle Book
Everything® Crosswords and Puzzles for Quote Lovers Book, $9.95
Everything® Crossword Challenge Book
Everything® Crosswords for the Beach Book, $9.95
Everything® Cryptic Crosswords Book, $9.95
Everything® Cryptograms Book, $9.95
Everything® Easy Crosswords Book
Everything® Easy Kakuro Book, $9.95
Everything® Easy Large-Print Crosswords Book
Everything® Games Book, 2nd Ed.
Everything® Giant Book of Crosswords
Everything® Giant Sudoku Book, $9.95
Everything® Giant Word Search Book
Everything® Kakuro Challenge Book, $9.95
Everything® Large-Print Crossword Challenge Book
Everything® Large-Print Crosswords Book
Everything® Large-Print Travel Crosswords Book
Everything® Lateral Thinking Puzzles Book, $9.95
Everything® Literary Crosswords Book, $9.95
Everything® Mazes Book
Everything® Memory Booster Puzzles Book, $9.95

Everything® Movie Crosswords Book, $9.95
Everything® Music Crosswords Book, $9.95
Everything® Online Poker Book
Everything® Pencil Puzzles Book, $9.95
Everything® Poker Strategy Book
Everything® Pool & Billiards Book
Everything® Puzzles for Commuters Book, $9.95
Everything® Puzzles for Dog Lovers Book, $9.95
Everything® Sports Crosswords Book, $9.95
Everything® Test Your IQ Book, $9.95
Everything® Texas Hold 'Em Book, $9.95
Everything® Travel Crosswords Book, $9.95
Everything® Travel Mazes Book, $9.95
Everything® Travel Word Search Book, $9.95
Everything® TV Crosswords Book, $9.95
Everything® Word Games Challenge Book
Everything® Word Scramble Book
Everything® Word Search Book

HEALTH

Everything® Alzheimer's Book
Everything® Diabetes Book
Everything® First Aid Book, $9.95
Everything® Green Living Book
Everything® Health Guide to Addiction and Recovery
Everything® Health Guide to Adult Bipolar Disorder
Everything® Health Guide to Arthritis
Everything® Health Guide to Controlling Anxiety
Everything® Health Guide to Depression
Everything® Health Guide to Diabetes, 2nd Ed.
Everything® Health Guide to Fibromyalgia
Everything® Health Guide to Menopause, 2nd Ed.
Everything® Health Guide to Migraines
Everything® Health Guide to Multiple Sclerosis
Everything® Health Guide to OCD
Everything® Health Guide to PMS
Everything® Health Guide to Postpartum Care
Everything® Health Guide to Thyroid Disease
Everything® Hypnosis Book
Everything® Low Cholesterol Book
Everything® Menopause Book
Everything® Nutrition Book
Everything® Reflexology Book
Everything® Stress Management Book
Everything® Superfoods Book, $15.95

HISTORY

Everything® American Government Book
Everything® American History Book, 2nd Ed.
Everything® American Revolution Book, $15.95
Everything® Civil War Book
Everything® Freemasons Book
Everything® Irish History & Heritage Book
Everything® World War II Book, 2nd Ed.

HOBBIES

Everything® Candlemaking Book
Everything® Cartooning Book
Everything® Coin Collecting Book
Everything® Digital Photography Book, 2nd Ed.

Everything® Drawing Book
Everything® Family Tree Book, 2nd Ed.
Everything® Guide to Online Genealogy, $15.95
Everything® Knitting Book
Everything® Knots Book
Everything® Photography Book
Everything® Quilting Book
Everything® Sewing Book
Everything® Soapmaking Book, 2nd Ed.
Everything® Woodworking Book

HOME IMPROVEMENT

Everything® Feng Shui Book
Everything® Feng Shui Decluttering Book, $9.95
Everything® Fix-It Book
Everything® Green Living Book
Everything® Home Decorating Book
Everything® Home Storage Solutions Book
Everything® Homebuilding Book
Everything® Organize Your Home Book, 2nd Ed.

KIDS' BOOKS

All titles are $7.95
Everything® Fairy Tales Book, $14.95
Everything® Kids' Animal Puzzle & Activity Book
Everything® Kids' Astronomy Book
Everything® Kids' Baseball Book, 5th Ed.
Everything® Kids' Bible Trivia Book
Everything® Kids' Bugs Book
Everything® Kids' Cars and Trucks Puzzle and Activity Book
Everything® Kids' Christmas Puzzle & Activity Book
Everything® Kids' Connect the Dots
    Puzzle and Activity Book
Everything® Kids' Cookbook, 2nd Ed.
Everything® Kids' Crazy Puzzles Book
Everything® Kids' Dinosaurs Book
Everything® Kids' Dragons Puzzle and Activity Book
Everything® Kids' Environment Book $7.95
Everything® Kids' Fairies Puzzle and Activity Book
Everything® Kids' First Spanish Puzzle and Activity Book
Everything® Kids' Football Book
Everything® Kids' Geography Book
Everything® Kids' Gross Cookbook
Everything® Kids' Gross Hidden Pictures Book
Everything® Kids' Gross Jokes Book
Everything® Kids' Gross Mazes Book
Everything® Kids' Gross Puzzle & Activity Book
Everything® Kids' Halloween Puzzle & Activity Book
Everything® Kids' Hanukkah Puzzle and Activity Book
Everything® Kids' Hidden Pictures Book
Everything® Kids' Horses Book
Everything® Kids' Joke Book
Everything® Kids' Knock Knock Book
Everything® Kids' Learning French Book
Everything® Kids' Learning Spanish Book
Everything® Kids' Magical Science Experiments Book
Everything® Kids' Math Puzzles Book
Everything® Kids' Mazes Book
Everything® Kids' Money Book, 2nd Ed.
Everything® Kids' Mummies, Pharaoh's, and Pyramids
    Puzzle and Activity Book
Everything® Kids' Nature Book
Everything® Kids' Pirates Puzzle and Activity Book
Everything® Kids' Presidents Book
Everything® Kids' Princess Puzzle and Activity Book
Everything® Kids' Puzzle Book

Everything® Kids' Racecars Puzzle and Activity Book
Everything® Kids' Riddles & Brain Teasers Book
Everything® Kids' Science Experiments Book
Everything® Kids' Sharks Book
Everything® Kids' Soccer Book
Everything® Kids' Spelling Book
Everything® Kids' Spies Puzzle and Activity Book
Everything® Kids' States Book
Everything® Kids' Travel Activity Book
Everything® Kids' Word Search Puzzle and Activity Book

LANGUAGE

Everything® Conversational Japanese Book with CD, $19.95
Everything® French Grammar Book
Everything® French Phrase Book, $9.95
Everything® French Verb Book, $9.95
Everything® German Phrase Book, $9.95
Everything® German Practice Book with CD, $19.95
Everything® Inglés Book
Everything® Intermediate Spanish Book with CD, $19.95
Everything® Italian Phrase Book, $9.95
Everything® Italian Practice Book with CD, $19.95
Everything® Learning Brazilian Portuguese Book with CD, $19.95
Everything® Learning French Book with CD, 2nd Ed., $19.95
Everything® Learning German Book
Everything® Learning Italian Book
Everything® Learning Latin Book
Everything® Learning Russian Book with CD, $19.95
Everything® Learning Spanish Book
Everything® Learning Spanish Book with CD, 2nd Ed., $19.95
Everything® Russian Practice Book with CD, $19.95
Everything® Sign Language Book, $15.95
Everything® Spanish Grammar Book
Everything® Spanish Phrase Book, $9.95
Everything® Spanish Practice Book with CD, $19.95
Everything® Spanish Verb Book, $9.95
Everything® Speaking Mandarin Chinese Book with CD, $19.95

MUSIC

Everything® Bass Guitar Book with CD, $19.95
Everything® Drums Book with CD, $19.95
Everything® Guitar Book with CD, 2nd Ed., $19.95
Everything® Guitar Chords Book with CD, $19.95
Everything® Guitar Scales Book with CD, $19.95
Everything® Harmonica Book with CD, $15.95
Everything® Home Recording Book
Everything® Music Theory Book with CD, $19.95
Everything® Reading Music Book with CD, $19.95
Everything® Rock & Blues Guitar Book with CD, $19.95
Everything® Rock & Blues Piano Book with CD, $19.95
Everything® Rock Drums Book with CD, $19.95
Everything® Singing Book with CD, $19.95
Everything® Songwriting Book

NEW AGE

Everything® Astrology Book, 2nd Ed.
Everything® Birthday Personology Book
Everything® Celtic Wisdom Book, $15.95
Everything® Dreams Book, 2nd Ed.
Everything® Law of Attraction Book, $15.95
Everything® Love Signs Book, $9.95
Everything® Love Spells Book, $9.95
Everything® Palmistry Book
Everything® Psychic Book
Everything® Reiki Book

Everything® Sex Signs Book, $9.95
Everything® Spells & Charms Book, 2nd Ed.
Everything® Tarot Book, 2nd Ed.
Everything® Toltec Wisdom Book
Everything® Wicca & Witchcraft Book, 2nd Ed.

PARENTING

Everything® Baby Names Book, 2nd Ed.
Everything® Baby Shower Book, 2nd Ed.
Everything® Baby Sign Language Book with DVD
Everything® Baby's First Year Book
Everything® Birthing Book
Everything® Breastfeeding Book
Everything® Father-to-Be Book
Everything® Father's First Year Book
Everything® Get Ready for Baby Book, 2nd Ed.
Everything® Get Your Baby to Sleep Book, $9.95
Everything® Getting Pregnant Book
Everything® Guide to Pregnancy Over 35
Everything® Guide to Raising a One-Year-Old
Everything® Guide to Raising a Two-Year-Old
Everything® Guide to Raising Adolescent Boys
Everything® Guide to Raising Adolescent Girls
Everything® Mother's First Year Book
Everything® Parent's Guide to Childhood Illnesses
Everything® Parent's Guide to Children and Divorce
Everything® Parent's Guide to Children with ADD/ADHD
Everything® Parent's Guide to Children with Asperger's
    Syndrome
Everything® Parent's Guide to Children with Anxiety
Everything® Parent's Guide to Children with Asthma
Everything® Parent's Guide to Children with Autism
Everything® Parent's Guide to Children with Bipolar Disorder
Everything® Parent's Guide to Children with Depression
Everything® Parent's Guide to Children with Dyslexia
Everything® Parent's Guide to Children with Juvenile Diabetes
Everything® Parent's Guide to Children with OCD
Everything® Parent's Guide to Positive Discipline
Everything® Parent's Guide to Raising Boys
Everything® Parent's Guide to Raising Girls
Everything® Parent's Guide to Raising Siblings
Everything® Parent's Guide to Raising Your
    Adopted Child
Everything® Parent's Guide to Sensory Integration Disorder
Everything® Parent's Guide to Tantrums
Everything® Parent's Guide to the Strong-Willed Child
Everything® Parenting a Teenager Book
Everything® Potty Training Book, $9.95
Everything® Pregnancy Book, 3rd Ed.
Everything® Pregnancy Fitness Book
Everything® Pregnancy Nutrition Book
Everything® Pregnancy Organizer, 2nd Ed., $16.95
Everything® Toddler Activities Book
Everything® Toddler Book
Everything® Tween Book
Everything® Twins, Triplets, and More Book

PETS

Everything® Aquarium Book
Everything® Boxer Book
Everything® Cat Book, 2nd Ed.
Everything® Chihuahua Book
Everything® Cooking for Dogs Book
Everything® Dachshund Book
Everything® Dog Book, 2nd Ed.
Everything® Dog Grooming Book

Everything® Dog Obedience Book
Everything® Dog Owner's Organizer, $16.95
Everything® Dog Training and Tricks Book
Everything® German Shepherd Book
Everything® Golden Retriever Book
Everything® Horse Book, 2nd Ed., $15.95
Everything® Horse Care Book
Everything® Horseback Riding Book
Everything® Labrador Retriever Book
Everything® Poodle Book
Everything® Pug Book
Everything® Puppy Book
Everything® Small Dogs Book
Everything® Tropical Fish Book
Everything® Yorkshire Terrier Book

REFERENCE

Everything® American Presidents Book
Everything® Blogging Book
Everything® Build Your Vocabulary Book, $9.95
Everything® Car Care Book
Everything® Classical Mythology Book
Everything® Da Vinci Book
Everything® Einstein Book
Everything® Enneagram Book
Everything® Etiquette Book, 2nd Ed.
Everything® Family Christmas Book, $15.95
Everything® Guide to C. S. Lewis & Narnia
Everything® Guide to Divorce, 2nd Ed., $15.95
Everything® Guide to Edgar Allan Poe
Everything® Guide to Understanding Philosophy
Everything® Inventions and Patents Book
Everything® Jacqueline Kennedy Onassis Book
Everything® John F. Kennedy Book
Everything® Mafia Book
Everything® Martin Luther King Jr. Book
Everything® Pirates Book
Everything® Private Investigation Book
Everything® Psychology Book
Everything® Public Speaking Book, $9.95
Everything® Shakespeare Book, 2nd Ed.

RELIGION

Everything® Angels Book
Everything® Bible Book
Everything® Bible Study Book with CD, $19.95
Everything® Buddhism Book
Everything® Catholicism Book
Everything® Christianity Book
Everything® Gnostic Gospels Book
Everything® Hinduism Book, $15.95
Everything® History of the Bible Book
Everything® Jesus Book
Everything® Jewish History & Heritage Book
Everything® Judaism Book
Everything® Kabbalah Book
Everything® Koran Book
Everything® Mary Book
Everything® Mary Magdalene Book
Everything® Prayer Book

Everything® Saints Book, 2nd Ed.
Everything® Torah Book
Everything® Understanding Islam Book
Everything® Women of the Bible Book
Everything® World's Religions Book

SCHOOL & CAREERS

Everything® Career Tests Book
Everything® College Major Test Book
Everything® College Survival Book, 2nd Ed.
Everything® Cover Letter Book, 2nd Ed.
Everything® Filmmaking Book
Everything® Get-a-Job Book, 2nd Ed.
Everything® Guide to Being a Paralegal
Everything® Guide to Being a Personal Trainer
Everything® Guide to Being a Real Estate Agent
Everything® Guide to Being a Sales Rep
Everything® Guide to Being an Event Planner
Everything® Guide to Careers in Health Care
Everything® Guide to Careers in Law Enforcement
Everything® Guide to Government Jobs
Everything® Guide to Starting and Running a Catering Business
Everything® Guide to Starting and Running a Restaurant
Everything® Guide to Starting and Running a Retail Store
Everything® Job Interview Book, 2nd Ed.
Everything® New Nurse Book
Everything® New Teacher Book
Everything® Paying for College Book
Everything® Practice Interview Book
Everything® Resume Book, 3rd Ed.
Everything® Study Book

SELF-HELP

Everything® Body Language Book
Everything® Dating Book, 2nd Ed.
Everything® Great Sex Book
Everything® Guide to Caring for Aging Parents, $15.95
Everything® Self-Esteem Book
Everything® Self-Hypnosis Book, $9.95
Everything® Tantric Sex Book

SPORTS & FITNESS

Everything® Easy Fitness Book
Everything® Fishing Book
Everything® Guide to Weight Training, $15.95
Everything® Krav Maga for Fitness Book
Everything® Running Book, 2nd Ed.
Everything® Triathlon Training Book, $15.95

TRAVEL

Everything® Family Guide to Coastal Florida
Everything® Family Guide to Cruise Vacations
Everything® Family Guide to Hawaii
Everything® Family Guide to Las Vegas, 2nd Ed.
Everything® Family Guide to Mexico
Everything® Family Guide to New England, 2nd Ed.

Everything® Family Guide to New York City, 3rd Ed.
Everything® Family Guide to Northern California and Lake Tahoe
Everything® Family Guide to RV Travel & Campgrounds
Everything® Family Guide to the Caribbean
Everything® Family Guide to the Disneyland® Resort, California Adventure® Universal Studios®, and the Anaheim Area, 2nd Ed.
Everything® Family Guide to the Walt Disney World Resort®, Universal Studios®, and Greater Orlando, 5th Ed.
Everything® Family Guide to Timeshares
Everything® Family Guide to Washington D.C., 2nd Ed.

WEDDINGS

Everything® Bachelorette Party Book, $9.95
Everything® Bridesmaid Book, $9.95
Everything® Destination Wedding Book
Everything® Father of the Bride Book, $9.95
Everything® Green Wedding Book, $15.95
Everything® Groom Book, $9.95
Everything® Jewish Wedding Book, 2nd Ed., $15.95
Everything® Mother of the Bride Book, $9.95
Everything® Outdoor Wedding Book
Everything® Wedding Book, 3rd Ed.
Everything® Wedding Checklist, $9.95
Everything® Wedding Etiquette Book, $9.95
Everything® Wedding Organizer, 2nd Ed., $16.95
Everything® Wedding Shower Book, $9.95
Everything® Wedding Vows Book, 3rd Ed., $9.95
Everything® Wedding Workout Book
Everything® Weddings on a Budget Book, 2nd Ed., $9.95

WRITING

Everything® Creative Writing Book
Everything® Get Published Book, 2nd Ed.
Everything® Grammar and Style Book, 2nd Ed.
Everything® Guide to Magazine Writing
Everything® Guide to Writing a Book Proposal
Everything® Guide to Writing a Novel
Everything® Guide to Writing Children's Books
Everything® Guide to Writing Copy
Everything® Guide to Writing Graphic Novels
Everything® Guide to Writing Research Papers
Everything® Guide to Writing a Romance Novel, $15.95
Everything® Improve Your Writing Book, 2nd Ed.
Everything® Writing Poetry Book